Heroes, Villains & Victims

OF HULL AND THE EAST RIDING

Heroes, Villains & Victims

OF HULL AND THE EAST RIDING

STUART RUSSELL

breedon **books**
PUBLISHING

First published in Great Britain in 2003 by
The Breedon Books Publishing Company Limited
Breedon House, 3 The Parker Centre,
Derby, DE21 4SZ.

ISBN 1 85983 367 5

Printed and bound by Butler & Tanner,
Frome, Somerset, England.

Cover printing by Lawrence-Allen Colour Printers,
Weston-super-Mare, Somerset, England.

Contents

Author's note

The stories in this book are true. All those
referred to in the following pages lived and
their exploits are taken from published
documentation. In some cases first-person
accounts have been used to aid narrative.

Preface

THIS book is about people. Some were good, philanthropists aware of their social responsibilities and determined to work for the betterment of mankind. But others were to leave their marks on the lives of others for very different reasons.

And some were the victims, the innocents who found themselves in the wrong place at the wrong time.

Any age has its heroes and its villains. The deeds of the most daring or notorious are well recorded. There are many more whose exploits are also well worthy of recording, but whose influences on their fellow men have been consigned to the dustbin of history.

In the following pages we meet some of those people. Their adventures and their misdemeanors reflect the ages in which they lived. They are now a part of all our histories. But without them and others like them the stories of our towns and villages would be that much poorer.

A soldier's tale

A light summer breeze fanned through the packed terraces, whispering down dank and dingy alleyways where whole families eked out a miserable, hungry existence in cramped and filthy rooms without even the most basic of life's essentials.

Children scampered on broken and uneven paving stones in narrow streets littered with decaying debris. Women gossiped on the pavements oblivious to the heavy stench which hung over the town and men lounged on street corners or, when they could beg or steal the money to buy it, supped ale and cheap gin in the numerous taverns.

The growing town of Hull was little better than a gigantic slum. Hygiene was, for most of its people, unknown. Drinking water was usually fouled. Homes were crumbling hovels, without furniture or comforts. To live was a battle fought from day to day...

The room in which the old woman lived was off the Market Place and was neither better nor worse than any of the hundreds of similar buildings to be found in mid 19th-century Hull. It was filthy, dark and devoid of furniture save for a straw mattress and a broken chair. In wet weather rain poured through holes in the roof where tiles had been torn away by gales. The only window, tiny and totally inadequate, was broken, the hole being stuffed with a dirty piece of rag in a futile attempt to keep out the flies.

The woman's foul and stinking home was at the end of a dark and narrow passageway which had over the years been defiled by animals of varying species. Closed in on every side, the buildings reached through this decaying entrance offered just 20 rooms, which were at any one time occupied by at least 120 people. Most of them would die well before they reached their 30th year. And all would bear the hallmarks of deprivation. Unwashed and dressed only in rags, their hair lank and filthy, they carried the haggard look of the undernourished. Food came only through begging, stealing or scavenging. Suicide was commonplace.

On that hot July morning the woman lay on the boards of the floor, unable to raise the strength to crawl to her bed. She shivered violently despite the warmth and she coughed, a deep, harsh, wracking bark, that tore at her weakened lungs. In the heat of a summer's day it took her hours to die as the spasms which shook her thin body became more frequent and more severe. Down her grimy face, unwashed for weeks, cold sweat ran in rivulets as slowly and inevitably the moment drew closer.

Relief came in the early evening, the agony at last giving way to the darkness that enveloped her. And as night crept over Hull the disease which had claimed her was spreading its tentacles throughout the town. Soon the terrible presence of cholera would take almost 2,000 lives and bring fear and death on a scale the like of which had not been seen since the Plague had last struck the town over two centuries earlier.

When the Revd James Sibree first arrived in Hull from London he was not impressed by what he saw. This kindly nonconformist preacher had never really wanted to leave his good living in the south but had, on the orders of his superiors, headed north to supervise the creation of a new church in Hull. Despite his initial reservations his two-month engagement was to last half a century.

Sibree, a native of Somerset, had departed from London at 4pm on 8 July 1831 on an express four-horse coach. The 170-mile journey took him to Barton, on the southern bank of the River Humber, where he arrived at 6pm the following day before boarding a small and inconvenient steam boat to Hull.

It proved to be a town for which he had scant regard – at least initially. He made his views clear in letters to his mother, telling her they were coming from 'the fag end of the earth'. However, he quickly proved a success, being popular with the people and achieving what he had been sent to do. When he was asked to remain in Hull for a stipend of £100 per year he accepted.

On 2 June 1847, almost two years after leaving the ferry from Barton, James Sibree was among a group of selected guests who were invited to attend the official opening of the Hull General Cemetery on Spring Bank. He was by then its chaplain.

At the entrance lodge some of the great and good of the town looked on in proud silence as the Mayor, Mr B.M. Jalland, laid the first stone. It was a significant moment, one which moved a local newspaper to report:

All present seemed to hail the opening of this extensive plot of ground for the purpose of interment as a real and great blessing and virtually to bid a glad farewell to those burial places where a grave cannot be dug without a profane and disgusting inroad on others and a revelation of scenes from which humanity shudderingly recoils.

Under the guidance of its superintendent, Mr John Shields, the new cemetery was imposing to say the least. It boasted a great variety of shrubs and trees, being 'a colourful place with people planting flowers around graves'. Rare moths and butterflies were found there and 'birds of the sweetest song, among them thrushes, blackbirds and woodlark, abounded'.

The monument to the victims of the cholera outbreak of 1849. One in 43 of the population of Hull fell victim to the disease.

Two more years passed before the fateful summer of 1849 saw Mr Sibree back amid those same and by now familiar surroundings, engaged on work which was to be etched on his memory for ever. It was the time when cholera struck, and, as he would later recall, it brought the darkest days of his life.

For up to 12 hours a day, often in the darkness of summer nights illuminated only by the flickering flames of candles, Sibree was on duty at the cemetery he came to love as the processions wound their way towards the burial plots. He was later to write:

Persons were seen crowding the entrance gates of the cemetery early in the morning, long before the wearied superintendent was up to order graves for friends and relatives who had died during the night, and, sad to relate, in many instances these informants were themselves, in a day or two, called to pass through the dark valley so short was the summons.

The most oppressive and trying scenes to myself were those when the sun had gone down and there was no moon to lighten the darkness at the grave and there was only the lantern dimly burning to help in the dreary work.

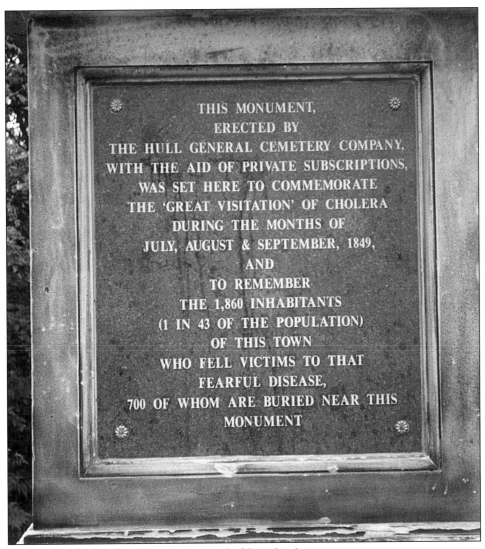

THIS MONUMENT,
ERECTED BY
THE HULL GENERAL CEMETERY COMPANY,
WITH THE AID OF PRIVATE SUBSCRIPTIONS,
WAS SET HERE TO COMMEMORATE
THE 'GREAT VISITATION' OF CHOLERA
DURING THE MONTHS OF
JULY, AUGUST & SEPTEMBER, 1849,
AND
TO REMEMBER
THE 1,860 INHABITANTS
(1 IN 43 OF THE POPULATION)
OF THIS TOWN
WHO FELL VICTIMS TO THAT
FEARFUL DISEASE,
700 OF WHOM ARE BURIED NEAR THIS
MONUMENT

The plaque on the obelisk recording the grim details of the outbreak.

Sometimes as many as five or six mourning trains crowded the gravel walkways:

> ... *while during the day, at some periods, the trains occupied the entire space between Beverley Road and the cemetery gates. None of those residing on the great thoroughfares could move out of their doors or look out of their windows without seeing men constantly passing with coffins on their shoulders or funeral trains on their way.*

At night the scenes were the most saddening. Tar barrels were set on fire in the streets which threw a ghostly glare all around. From the testimony of the police and medical men, I gathered that at any one period the night was as the day.

Most of the victims were young. And the vast majority of those being interred were poor, records showing that of those who died 1,738 were from the 'labouring class' while only 122 came from the 'gentry, traders and well to do classes'.

The social effects were devastating. Some parents lost all their children and some children lost both their parents. One family, that of a brickmaker living in Ropery Street, was eliminated – all eight of them dying within a few days of each other. A commercial traveller was suddenly taken ill at the inn where he was staying and was carried to his grave without a single mourner. An aged widow residing in a miserable garrett in Pig Alley died alone, those living below her being too concerned about their own wellbeing to even consider her. When they did they found her 'shrivelled body, awfully discoloured, cold, stiff and dead with her knees doubled up by the agonising cramp. She could not be laid out and the undertaker and his men were unable, without violence, to straighten the limbs, so in place of a coffin they made a sort of triangular box suited to the death shape of her body. It was an unsightly thing, such as had never been made before.'

And so it went on, day after terrible day.

As the processions of death continued they were watched by Robert Colbourne with calm detachment. It was for him, given the task of acting as cemetery gatekeeper during the emergency, a by now familiar sight. Initially finding it harrowing, he had grown accustomed to the weeping and wailing of the mourners, to the rattle of the death carts as they made their way past the gatehouse, to the awfulness of what was happening.

At 15 years old Robert, a bright and happy boy 'tall and of thin make' was witness to a piece of Hull history. It did not fail to make an impact upon him.

It was as he watched the mourners filing past that Robert first became aware of one of them, a boy not much older than himself, obviously upset, but controlling his emotions as he walked slowly towards the burial plots. Smart in his military uniform he was mourning his father, mother and sister. When the boy left following the short and simple ceremony Colbourne murmured a brief message of commiseration to him as he passed through the gates, the same few simple words he was told to utter to everyone who visited the cemetery. They were to prove to be words that would alter the course of his life.

The Crimea, 1854

Over the battlefield the stench of death hung heavy in the evening air. An eerie silence was punctuated by the cries of the injured and dying as the teams of soldiers and medical men moved slowly among the mass of bodies of men from both sides of the conflict.

The earth was pitted with shell holes. Not a tree, nor single blade of grass was visible across the quagmire of men and mud that had once been lush meadowland.

A chill wind crept across this bleak and barren landscape, fanning outwards to the plain. And with it came the first flurries of snow.

In the trench a group of British soldiers gathered around their apology for a fire, the last few scraps of wood giving little light and even less heat. Some of them were on the edge of madness, driven to live like beasts, denied proper food or rest for months. Their clothes were in rags, their boots torn apart at the seams. What had once been the proud, bright uniform of the British Army was almost indistinguishable.

'Jesus, it's cold.'

'Aye and gettin' colder.'

The grumble came from a thousand throats a thousand times a day. And they all knew that from now on as winter drew nearer it could only grow colder.

Robert Colbourne was lucky. Although faring no better than thousands of others he was at least still alive and uninjured. Oblivious by now to the conditions, he and the men with him had come to accept what they were convinced was their fate. Morale had long since evaporated. Now they fought man for man to survive, but for most it was a pointless exercise. As the whirling flakes of snow danced he pulled the scraps of clothing tightly around him, appreciating that it was a gesture of utter futility, and rose from the fire to pick his way through the debris of war to the horse which stood nearby, once a proud charger, now the most pitiable sight he had ever seen. Months before this wreckling had been handsome and impressive like the men who rode him. Now he beggared description, a living skeleton, emaciated, filthy and unwanted. He had no mane and no tail. His deep set eyes were glaring and ferocious.

The creature was covered in thick mud which had caked on to his flesh. He stood shivering in the chill of evening up to his knees in the cloying filth, tied to what had once been a shrub but which was now a bundle of withered branches.

Colbourne edged past the beast, wary that it might kick out in an act of defiant desperation, and forced himself to think of other things. Somehow the plight of the horse, no different to any one of many hundreds of beasts and men strewn across the battlefields, had moved him momentarily and despair welled inside him. He doubted now if he would ever see his home in Hull or his family again.

It had seemed such a great opportunity when the young man whom he had met at the cemetery gates on Spring Bank, and to whom he had muttered those words of commiseration, had struck up a conversation which had led to him joining the 50th Regiment of Foot – the Queen's Own.

After that life had been a whirlwind of activity as preparations were made for war. Russia, ever anxious to expand her territories, faced the combined opposition of England, France and Turkey. By September 1854, 50,000 English and French troops were in the Crimea squaring up for what was to become one of the greatest military scandals in British military history. Young Robert was a part of it, witnessing the appalling slaughter on both sides at three major battles – Balaclava, Inkerman and Alma – and in the process being awarded two medals and four bars for his dedication and bravery. Despite the terrible privations, forever cold, hungry and thirsty, living shoeless and in rags, he remained a loyal soldier. Until, that is, the dawning of that fateful day when, after 72 hours in the entrenchment of Sebastopol he was sent 'on a very small allowance of rations' down to the harbour at Balaclava with two packhorses to collect stores.

Balaclava was best described by a 19th-century writer who said that the village – by now little more than a collection of huts – had become 'quite a metropolis'. In fact, at that time there was not another village in the world which, for its size, could have shown the same amount of business and excitement.

Before the war Balaclava had been an attractive fishing village and resort lying in the shadow of steep cliffs and used by the people of Sebastopol as a friendly and charming holiday destination. The village had at that time green tiled cottages covered in honeysuckle and clematis and a deep and pleasant harbour where ships could moor alongside well-built wharves.

By the time Robert Colbourne arrived Balaclava resembled no other community on earth. 'It was jammed with men and beasts and vehicles and supplies as guns and armour were dragged from ships to the heights overlooking Sebastopol,' said one writer:

The motley crowd that was perpetually wading about in the piles of uneatable eatables which had been unloaded there was something beyond description. The very ragged, gaunt and hungry looking men with matted beards and moustaches, features grimed with dirt and great coats stiff with successive layers of mud, whose whole appearance spoke of toil and suffering, were picked soldiers from different foot regiments, strong and selected men to carry provisions for the rest of the camp.

When provisions were available, that is. For shambolic organisation had led to food being left to rot where it was unloaded.

There was no sanitation, no attempt to hygienically deal with the dead and the dying who were taken to the village. In the harbour amputated legs and arms from injured soldiers, many of them still in sleeves or trousers, floated in the mud to the scummy surface and men 'took to any cheap liquor they could find to ease their misery'.

By now Robert Colbourne was hardened to such scenes as he picked his way through the morass to the harbour. And it was as he scanned the rows of waiting ships that he began to realise that several of them were from Hull. Inquisitive, he boarded one, engaged a young member of its crew in conversation and a couple of hours later had accepted an invitation to go for drinks in a French canteen. What he did not reckon on was the devastating effect that strong alcohol would have on his thin, emaciated body. It wasn't long before he was insensible.

The young sailors, who were due to leave on the next tide, tried to revive him but without success. When Robert Colbourne finally came to his senses the ship was at sea. He was a deserter.

The Old Town, Hull

In a peaceful corner of the Market Place a weary policeman sat down to rest, perching precariously on the high – and strong – hat which was a feature of the force's uniform. It was springtime and the chill, dank days of winter were already a fading memory.

Sun filtered through light clouds to bring cheer to the bustling streets but the policeman was unaware of the fact. He was tired after long hours on duty and he yawned as he dozed. That day he was one of about two dozen members of the force on duty in the streets of central Hull. All were dressed in similar fashion, with swallow-tail coats. They each carried a truncheon 'of the most formidable size'.

As he slumbered in his ungainly position the man was brought to his senses by a light tap on his shoulder. He awakened to find it was that of a young woman. He was instantly aware of the smell of gin upon her breath. But the story she told made PC John Withington sit up with a jerk, rise to don his high hat and set off with her running behind him to a house in another part of the area – Salthouse Lane.

To clear his path as he hurried on his way PC Withington waved his rattle, which created an 'unmistakable and hideous' sound. In the lane he stopped suddenly outside the house known as No.34 Gibson's Buildings, pausing momentarily before hammering on the door, shouting as he did so 'Police, Police, open up...'

The door opened to reveal a slightly-built woman. 'Yes, what is it? What do you want?' The voice was thin and nervous.

'Is this the home of Robert Colbourne?' The policeman's voice was loud and strident. Without being asked he pushed the woman to one side and marched into the house. The woman followed him as he first glanced around the tiny living room before rushing up the stairs and into a small bedroom at the rear of the building. There he found a young man hurriedly dressing in a vain bid to leave.

Two hours later, in the ugly fortress that was the Parliament Street Police Station, Robert Colbourne, soldier with the 50th Regiment of Foot and deserter from the British Army in the Crimea, was under interrogation. For the next seven years all he would know were the walls of prison.

As he tried to answer the questions the police threw aggressively at him throughout a long and difficult interview session, only a few hundred yards away a young woman was among the pack of drinkers at a Market Place tavern. For once she had money to spend, a whole guinea handed to her as the reward for the capture of Robert Colbourne. As she sipped the cheap gin she reflected that it had not been all that hard to inform on him, even though she was his sister-in-law.

The interrogation brought from Colbourne a strange story of what had happened to him since that fateful day when he drunkenly boarded the ship in Balaclava harbour.

James Sibree takes up the story:

The sailors were worried and through fear of the consequences took him on their ship and hid him among the coals of the bunkers.

He awoke at sea, a deserter before the enemy, an act punishable by death.

On the ship's arrival at Varna, the sailors, fearing detection, lowered a boat while their captain slept and put Robert ashore, giving him 60 piastras to help him on his way.

After reaching Constantinople he eventually returned to Hull where his dreams of security and happiness soon turned to nightmare.

County Cork, Ireland

Robert Colbourne stood stiffly to attention as the court martial considered its verdict. The date was 28 February 1856 and he shivered in grim anticipation of what was to come. Since his arrest he had been taken to Fermoy, in County Cork, and held in a cold and meagre cell awaiting his fate.

The hearing was brief, but fair, the court deciding that the sentence for his desertion should be death. But after pleas on Robert's behalf – they were particularly impressed by the fact that he had won two medals and four bars for bravery in battle – the sentence was reduced to one of penal servitude for life 'in consideration of his youth and inexperience'.

Following the decision his days in Fermoy were few and before long he was marched under escort to Dublin and a cell in the notorious Mountjoy Prison, where, in letters to both Mr Sibree and his relatives in Hull, he started to tell of his life and treatment:

... On my arrival I was stripped and thrown into a lightsome cell there to wait till they brought me a suit of clothes along with a mask. That black mask I wore for 12 months.

This government prison is on the separate system but the terms of separation are greatly reduced on account of so many men committing suicide.

I have myself often gone down on my knees and prayed to God to let the roof fall in and crush me, for when a man once enters that place he is buried alive, for you never see anyone's face except four persons, the governor, doctor, chaplain and warden. When out for exercise, all masked, we are marched in a circle 10 paces in the rear of each other. Silence is strictly observed and if broken by any prisoner he is thrown into a dark cell for three days and nights on bread and water. If ever there is a place of misery in the world it is Mountjoy Prison.

But what happened in Mountjoy was only the beginning compared to what lay ahead. On 13 March 1857 Colbourne was moved – to Spike Island, in County Cork.

Spike Island Prison

It had looked a 'dainty tit-bit'. And despite the orders Robert Colbourne just could not resist bending to pick up the few shreds of tobacco which lay on the paving of the exercise yard. Inevitably he had been seen and marched before the prison governor. And now he faced his punishment, in a dismal, dank and stinking cell. A large black rat scurried across the floor startling him momentarily. Water dripped incessantly through the roof, splashing into muddy puddles. Robert Colbourne had reached the depths of despair.

He was in solitary confinement for 21 days with only bread to eat and cold water to drink. And there was no hope whatever of escape.

Spike Island was occupied solely by the prison and its outbuildings. It was surrounded by the waters of the River Lee and the nearest land lay half a mile away. To the men held on the island it could as easily have been a hundred miles.

In a letter home Colbourne had told of his despair. 'Often I have resolved and planned and replanned to reach that point, but it is watched day and night by soldiers. Only one man was ever known to escape, but he was taken by the crew of a coastguard boat just as he reached the other side.'

The men who shared this island hell were a mixed bunch. Among them were common criminals who rubbed shoulders with convicts originally from the higher ranks of life – one of them being a Scottish nobleman.

Some were well educated 'and had distinguished themselves in art and science'. But on Spike Island all suffered under the same brutal treatment meted out by the prison warders.

As James Sibree was later to write: 'Trifling acts of indiscretion such as receiving a newspaper, speaking impertinently to a tyrannical warder or picking up the smallest bit of tobacco were all visited with the utmost severity'.

And Colbourne could do nothing but reflect on his position:

This cell is under the ramparts and the water drops from the arched roof down upon the prisoner confined there. At night you have no bed or bedding excepting an old rug the turnkey throws in to you at nine o'clock and is taken away at five in the morning.

The punishment will try the stoutest heart that ever beat. Half a pound of

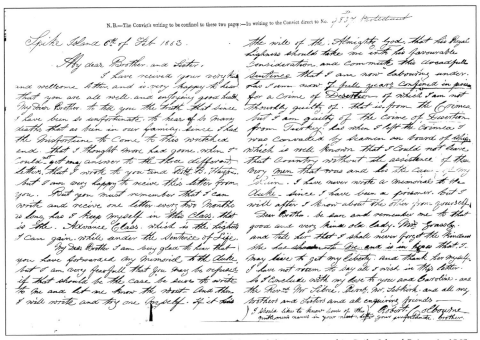

Robert Colbourne wrote this letter to his brother and sister while incarcerated in Spike Island Prison in 1863.

bread is given at six o'clock in the morning and another at six in the evening with a drink of cold water.

In cases of subordination men are punished by the Cat. Two drummers, out of the barracks at Cork, or boatswains from the guardship in front of Queenstown each give 25 lashes. The most cursed of all places, that is Spike Island. Many a time have I looked over at the green fields, then at the ships coming in and going out of the harbour. I sometimes thought I would kill one of the guards and so end my misery...

For over six years the young soldier endured these conditions, being allowed only occasionally to write home to his family in Hull. But from the depths of despair came hope.

The Old Town, Hull

The Revd James Sibree read slowly and carefully from the pile of letters handed to him by the middle-aged woman.

'You are asking me to help?' he inquired softly. She nodded. 'If you could, if only you

CONVICT ESTABLISHMENT, *Ireland*

SPIKE ISLAND. *6th of February '63*

Convicts are permitted to write one Letter on reception and another at the end of three months. They may also receive one Letter (pre-paid) every three months during their stay.

Matters of private importance to a Convict may be communicated at any time by Letter (pre-paid) to the Governor, who will inform the Convict thereof, if expedient.

In case of misconduct the privilege of receiving or writing a Letter may be forfeited for the time.

All Letters of an improper or idle tendency, either to or from Convicts, or containing slang or other objectionable expressions, will be suppressed. The permission to write and receive Letters is given to the Convicts for the purpose of enabling them to keep up a connection with their respectable friends, and not that they may hear the news of the day.

All Letters are read by the Governor and Chaplain and must be legibly written, and not crossed.

Neither clothes, money, nor any other articles are allowed to be received at the Prison, for the use of Convicts, except through the Governor; persons attempting otherwise to introduce any article to or for a Convict are liable to Fine or Imprisonment, and the Convict concerned is liable to be severely punished.

1,463. 1,000. 10. 62

Letter writing – and receiving – was a privilege. And all were read by the prison governor and chaplain. This notice to convicts was issued by the Spike Island authorities.

could. Something has to be done. Poor Bob, he's innocent really, it was just a mistake. His record proves he was a good soldier, he was given awards for bravery. He would never have deserted willingly, you know that.'

'Indeed I do,' said Sibree. 'I remember him well, from the days of the cholera. He was a good lad.'

The woman departed and Sibree settled down to think, recalling the moment many years later: 'She had heard that I had succeeded in rescuing another young soldier, the son of an officer who had died in India who had been condemned to penal servitude for insubordination in Corfu and had served a portion of his time on board the hulks in the Thames.'

As soon as Mrs Colbourne left his home he settled down to plan a campaign of action that would even involve royalty...

Spike Island Prison

Robert Colbourne sat with his head in his hands in deep anguish and despair. It was a despair reflected in a letter he wrote to his family, dated 6 February 1863. By then he was serving his seventh year in prison for 'a crime of which I am not thoroughly guilty'.

His letter said:

My dear Brother and Sister,
I have received your very kind and welcome letter and is very happy to hear that you are all well and enjoying good health.

My dear Brother, to tell you the truth, that since I have been so unfortunate to hear of so many deaths that has been in our family since I had the misfortune to come to this wretched end that I thought more had gone when I could not get any answer to the three different letters that I wrote to you, but I am very happy to receive this letter from you.

You must remember that I can write and receive one letter every two months as long as I can keep myself in this class – that is the advance class, which is the highest I can gain while under the sentence of life.

My dear Brother, I am very glad to hear that you have forwarded my memorial to the Duke (believed to be HRH Prince George of Cambridge), but I am very fearful that you will be refused.

If that should be the case be sure to write to me and let me know the worst and then I will write and try one myself...

The Old Town, Hull

A letter to Prince George had in fact been written by James Sibree giving Robert's case and all the mitigating circumstances surrounding it. Sibree wrote later: 'The answer was unfavourable.' Time passed by, the weeks becoming months. Nothing happened.

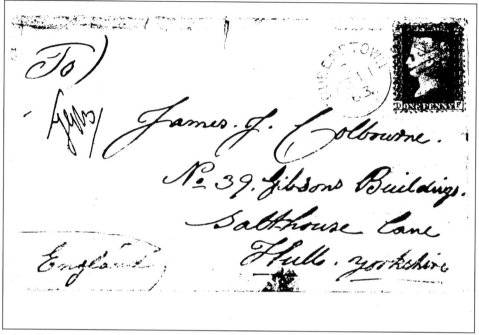

A letter from jail. Robert Colbourne's message to his family arrived in this envelope.

Sibree recalled: 'Then I induced my friend the Revd James Selkirk, who was Chaplain of the Hull Gaol, to forward a petition on his [Colbourne's] behalf to his Royal Highness.'

Again the reply was unfavourable. It said: 'I am directed by the Secretary of State to acquaint you that his Royal Highness, the Field Marshall Commanding-in-Chief sees no reason for recommending a commutation of the sentence of the court martial in the case of the offender.'

But Sibree was not a man who took defeat easily. He continued his campaign, again writing to Prince George, but this time never receiving a reply. 'The heart of Britain's princes was not, like that of the unjust judge in Our Lord's parable, to be wearied.'

All was not yet lost, however, and the longed for 'light and deliverance' was to come, although from an unexpected quarter. Sibree wrote:

> As soon as I knew of Robert Colbourne's imprisonment I opened a correspondence with him as often as prison rules admitted in which were words of encouragement and assurances that I was using all the means in my power for his release.

The letters were always read by the governor before they were seen by himself. The last of these was inquired for, and read by, one of the Inspectors of Her Majesty's Prisons at one of the monthly visitations.

I cannot remember what was written, but it awakened so much interest in the mind of the inspector that it was immediately forwarded – I presume with his report – to Dublin Castle for the perusal of the Earl of Carlisle, then Lord Lieutenant of Ireland.

This kind hearted nobleman was so moved as to despatch an order for the miserable convict's immediate reprieve. There is no reason to believe that this was the last act of mercy performed by his Lordship before the termination of his wise administration as the Viceroy of Ireland.

In his cell on Spike Island Robert Colbourne wept as the news of his release was broken to him. The years of beatings, near starvation and despair, which had driven him to the brink of suicide, were over.

And at last he went home to Hull, arriving with Mr Sibree at the door of the minister's home. Sibree would later write:

I cannot describe my own feelings, or the joy that filled all hearts when the tidings rang through my house – 'Robert is here! Poor Bob is come!' It was so sudden and unexpected. His sister led him within our doors for his poor mother had passed away from all earth's sorrows and it was pitiful to see in his looks and dazed manner and inability to speak for wonder to find himself where he was, what prison life and prison terrors had done for him.

His youth and manhood had been ground out of him. Tears of gladness were on every face as the wanderer kneeled down with me and my family in the middle of the room to render our thanks to the Great Deliverer...

Nothing more is known of Robert Colbourne following his release from prison.

James Sibree continued his work with the church in Hull. He died on at 2.45am on 27 December 1891 aged 86, the oldest nonconformist minister in the town. A newspaper obituary said of him: 'No man of Hull was better known than Mr Sibree.'

James Sibree was buried in the Hull General Cemetery where during his lifetime he had read the burial services for over 18,000 of his fellow citizens.

The thief

Port Jackson Harbour, Sydney, Australia

The man was tall, but age and events had taken their toll. Now he stooped, his back bent, his hair grey. But the eyes still reflected the inner soul, cunning and secretive.

In the heat of the day he worked steadily, the sweat running down his brow and blinding him as he wheeled load after heavy load of earth and stones. His body ached and he was hungry and thirsty. But his mind was fresh as he dreamed of days gone by.

As Snowden Dunhill worked under the relentless glare of the southern sun he remembered his childhood and the years beyond, recalling with crystal clarity the soft green Wolds running gently towards the basin of the River Humber, swirling along its muddy path towards the sea.

Ten thousand miles from the place he was now forced to call home he looked back a lifetime to recall the fields, the trees and the villages of the East Riding. With sadness he knew he would he would never see them again.

A tap on the shoulder broke his daydream, bringing him back to the harsh reality of convict life. And then the stranger's voice, soft and strange, but with an accent that was still familiar: 'Well, Snowden, how are you?'

He turned, touched his cap in a token of respect, and looked for the first time in over half a century into a face he had last seen gasping for breath on the bank of a moat in Spaldington, near Howden...

The peaked roofs of the Old Hall rose majestically above the cluster of cottages and farm buildings that comprised the village. Wind rifled through the tall trees and rooks spiralled high in the air above neat fields. The hall was surrounded by a wide and deep moat, built more for ornamental reasons than defensive ones. In a village with little else to offer them the water of the moat proved a natural magnet for the local boys.

As they darted about, chasing each other along the edge of the water, there was a sudden sharp cry as one of them fell into what was the deepest part of the entire moat. Struggling wildly, for he could not swim, the boy screamed in terror, vanishing below the surface only to rise again gasping for air.

As he fought for his life the others looked on in horrified disbelief, among them Snowden Dunhill, who would later recall:

> We saw the poor fellow sinking for the last time, and heard the horrid gargle of suffocation in his throat. I could restrain myself no longer and, though not more than six years old at the time, leaped headlong into the water. Seizing my senseless companion by some part of his dress, we struggled so effectually that both of us reached the opposite bank in safety, but he was nearly drowned...

It was a brave action to take and young Snowden's heroics undoubtedly earned him the highest praise. But still those who lived in Spaldington were under no illusions about another, less acceptable side to his character. For even as a boy Snowden Dunhill was an accomplished thief.

In Spaldington this idle, mischievous youngster on his own admission 'practised a variety of petty thefts, without being suspected'. It set him up well for what was to follow. Described as a highwayman by some, that was a profession he never actually adopted. But his reputation as a thief was unsurpassed.

One historian was later to write of him and his gang: 'The daring and extensive depredations of these vagabonds were astonishing and invested their chief with a mysterious and unenviable fame such as might attach to the character of the Rob Roy of the East Riding.'

Certainly Dunhill was an intelligent man, bright enough to read and write, tasks which he proved adept at doing, setting down his story in clear and concise form, and eventually having it published by William Pratt, of Howden, in 1834.

But perhaps he was not so bright when it came to women. For the one he married was Sarah Taylor, the widow of a man shot while carrying out a crime. And her influence on him played a significant role in shaping his future career. Of his marriage he was to write in his memoir *The Life of Snowden Dunhill*:

... Mine assuredly deepened the darkest shades of my character. It was not a connection of the heart, but almost one of fear, for the woman to whom I paid my addresses was the being who ruled me from the first moment of our acquaintance. Had it been my fortune to have met with an honest and industrious woman my destiny might have been different...

Sarah guaranteed that Snowden kept on stealing.

Steadily his 'business' built up, being operated out of a cottage in which the family lived on the road between Howden and Market Weighton, the chief recipients of his attentions being local farmers. It was, he was later to recall: 'The best situation that could have been chosen if the farmers had wished us to continue our system of plunder.' It was a system that would lead to the downfall of both him and his family.

Besides being expert at stealing – 'there was scarcely a barn or granary within several miles which I had not the means of entering when I chose' – Dunhill was also an expert horseman and had a love for his animals, although on his own admission there were occasions when 'one or two acts of apparent cruelty' were necessary, rising from the need for self-preservation rather than anything else.

There was one occasion when, while carrying a considerable sum of money, he was riding at full speed late at night. The moon was bright and trees lined the green sward of grass which ran along the side of the road. Dunhill would write later:

...I felt a soothing calmness spread over my soul which I cannot well account for or explain the cause of. My musings were suddenly cut short by a deep drawn sigh from my horse, then a slight shudder and the next moment he was dead under me. I raised his head, but all in vain. No trace of life remained.

Snowden completed his journey on foot, a distance of many miles.

Known throughout the area for his exploits he was a man who lived dangerously and accepted the hazards of his trade. This even included being shot. It happened during a raid on a house near Howden. The building stood near to the River Ouse and Snowden and his friends had laid on a boat to carry the goods they were about to steal down to Swinefleet.

But as soon as they started to approach the house in the dead of night things went horribly wrong. While crossing a garden at the back of the house Dunhill stepped on a piece of fencing which broke, the noise of it cracking causing a dog to bark and awakening the owner of the property.

Almost instantly a shot was fired from the upper part of the eastern end of the house. It hit him in the back and shoulders, knocking him to the ground. Dunhill wrote of the incident: 'I at length contrived with great difficulty to get upon my feet and with still greater exertion and much loss of blood I reached the boat, where I found my men in great consternation and alarm…'

He was taken to Howden, being almost insensible through pain and the loss of blood when he finally arrived, later recalling: 'By my desire they took me to the house of a medical man of my acquaintance, and knocked at his door. He soon came down and without asking a single question stripped me and during the night he extracted no fewer than 38 large shot corns from my back.'

It was an incident which left him with injuries from which he never really recovered. But it failed to stop him stealing.

A tall, large limbed man with light hair, round face and rather florid complexion, Dunhill, at the age of 40, had developed a touch of vanity in his character, comparing his looks to those of two rather more lawful celebrities, Sir Walter Scott and William Cobbet.

Without doubt crime helped Snowden to prosper. He owned two horses and kept greyhounds and carried with him a large canvas purse filled with money, which he would lend to members of the local farming community.

He was a family man, and Sarah, about eight years older than himself, gave birth to five children, two of them sons. They were a family to be avoided.

The historian James Sheahan in his *History of Hull*, published in 1866, described Snowden and his men as 'the terror of the [Howden] district'. He went on: 'It is but rare in the history of crime, dark as is the picture it presents, that we find such an aggregate of guilt, and such a weight of judicial infliction in connection with the history of one family as is associated with that of Snowden Dunhill.'

Dunhill's days in the East Riding were, however, to be curtailed, events coming to a head on 25 October 1812 in mid-afternoon when he responded to a knock on the cottage door which revealed a group of men, one carrying a justice's search warrant.

Despite a thorough going-over of his property the men could not find evidence against Snowden, a fact which not unnaturally gave him great pleasure. Not so pleased, though, was his wife. He would later recall: 'She, poor woman, swore she would take the law of them, threatened writs, indictments, justices and I know not what and I verily believed she would have inflicted summary vengeance on the head of the constable with the poker.'

Snowden's protestations of innocence were ignored. He was taken to York, then to London and back to York to be charged with theft. The punishment: seven years transportation.

He would later write: 'I was immediately conveyed back to my cell, and a few days afterwards I was forwarded to the hulks... I passed six years embittered by the most dreadful account of my family, every member of it in the remotest degree, having transgressed the laws of his country.'

His son, George, 'as handsome a young fellow as ever stepped upon show-leather', was transported, but could not stand the punishment and, for an unknown crime, was executed in Hobart Town, Van Dieman's Land. He had been transported from Beverley Sessions along with his mother and Rosa, Snowden's favourite daughter, who was committed and sentenced to confinement in York Castle for larceny. Rosa had two husbands, William McDowell, of Pontefract, and George Connor, of Leeds, both of whom were transported.

Another Dunhill daughter – Sarah – also fell foul of the law, being imprisoned in York and Beverley before, in 1828, being transported from Hull to New South Wales. Her crime was that of picking the pocket of a man named Scholfield and stealing a 'considerable sum' of money. According to Sheahan, she was humanely allowed to take her two infant children with her. Her *three* husbands – James Stanhope, alias 'One-armed Jem', Rhodes of Hull and James Crosland of the same town were each transported.

William, also a son of Snowden Dunhill, was sent to Australia by a court at York for a 14-year term but died on arrival. Snowden would say of him: 'He was the most promising of my family, and with different examples before him and good advice, he must have proved an ornament to society.'

Robert Taylor, a son of Mrs Dunhill's to a former husband, also received a transportation sentence.

As for Snowden, he served his seven years and came home to England, for a time living in De la Pole Court, Manor Street, Hull, conducting himself in his words 'with great propriety'. But he was lonely and distressed, looking ahead hopelessly to a bleak future. Slowly, probably inevitably, he formed dubious new relationships with people in Hull and in Lincolnshire.

They were not to last, however. He would later recall: 'I had heard much of the easy lives led by convicts in New South Wales and, moreover, some members of my family were already there and I felt impelled to make endeavour to join them.' He did not have long to wait, being arrested for a 'paltry crime', for which he was tried and convicted in 1825. This time he was transported for life. 'My character did the rest and readily procured for me that banishment from England on which I had set my heart,' he later wrote.

On arrival in Botany Bay the sought-after transportation did not live up to expectations. Snowden commenced 'in good earnest' the life of a slave, declaring that being 'hard worked, half starved, ill-fed and worse clothed is the fate of the hapless convict.'

Snowden Dunhill's sentence was eventually reduced and he then moved to Van Dieman's Land to join his wife and daughter. Sarah had become religious and taught at a day school. She also made pies which Snowden hawked around the town.

He appears to have been unhappy with his existence and started to drink heavily. He was seen by a traveller from the Howden area who would record that drinking was 'a vice which, by keeping him poor, will in all likelihood prevent him again seeing his native country.'

Rural Crime and Transportation: The Life of Snowden Dunhill, originally printed in 1835–6 is now re-published by Mr Pye (Books), of Howden.

Heroes of the people's war

Sixty years ago Britain was fighting to survive the greatest tyranny the world has ever known.

It was the people's war where, for the first time, women and children found themselves at the forefront of hostilities, as bombs brought home the horrors of modern conflict night after night, month after month. The people of Hull were no exception.

And it was also a time when ordinary people rose to the challenge and, in many cases, became heroes without whose efforts the conflict could never have been won.

Here we look back to those dark days with stories of heroism which brought glory to men and women called up to fight for their country's survival. They are superb tributes to the courage and fortitude of ordinary people when the odds were stacked against them.

Above the black calm of the lake the bomber flew steadily towards the climax of its mission, the roar of its engines bouncing off the menacing, cold waters.

Gently, calmly, Wing Commander Guy Gibson adjusted the controls, his brow furrowed in deep concentration as he struggled to keep the aircraft level at exactly 60ft above the surface. Ahead, the twin towers of the Mohne dam grew ever closer as the Lancaster bomber, AJ-G, pursued its lonely, dangerous course at a steady 240mph.

As the climactic moment approached each member of the crew pushed the natural sense of fear to the back of his mind to concentrate fully on the task which lay ahead.

Among them was the flight engineer, Flt Sgt John Pulford, a young Hull airman who, like his colleagues, was to earn a place in flying history.

Weeks of intense training lay behind this mission. Its importance was etched deep into the mind of every man on board. It was the night of Sunday 16 May 1943. The aircraft had left Scampton at precisely 21.39 hours, one of nine which would make the attack on the main targets of the Mohne and Eder dams. Five more crews would head for the Sorpe. The remaining five aircraft involved in the operation were to be used whenever they were needed.

As Gibson kept the aircraft steady as it roared across the Mohne lake flak came at them from the dam itself. The tension was intense. Then suddenly, came the shout: 'Bomb gone!' Gibson reacted instantly, pulling back on the stick. The Lancaster climbed slowly, almost reluctantly, rising over the dam's superstructure and into the blackness of the night...

He was later to recall that historic moment in his book *Enemy Coast Ahead*: 'We began to dive to the flat, ominous water. Over the front turret was the dam silhouetted against the haze of the Ruhr Valley. We could see the towers, we could see the sluices. We could see everything.'

As the aircraft neared the target Pulford 'began working on the speed. First he put on a little flap to slow us down, then he opened the throttles to get the air speed indicator exactly against the red mark...' wrote Gibson.

But the Germans were alerted by now and tracer flashed through the dark skies towards them. 'By now we were a few hundred yards away and I said quickly to Pulford under my breath "Better leave the throttles open now and stand by to pull me out of the seat if I get hit". As I glanced at him I thought he looked a little glum on hearing this...'

Gibson's bomb hit the target, but despite throwing up a huge cloud of spray which took several minutes to subside did not penetrate the dam. And so, one after another, the aircraft roared in to attack. Finally the wall went.

'There was a great breach one hundred yards across and the water, looking like stirred porridge in the moonlight, was gushing out and rolling into the Ruhr Valley towards the industrial centres of Germany's Third Reich. We began to shout and scream and act like madmen over the RT, for this was a tremendous sight, a sight which probably no man will ever see again,' said Gibson.

The Mohne raid was over. But for Gibson and his crew there was still more to come as they then moved on to lead the raid on the Eder dam, which took them some time to find owing to thick fog. That, too, was breached '...as if a giant hand had punched a hole in cardboard, the whole thing collapsed'.

It was a superbly executed operation, a raid carried out with determination and immense skill in the face of terrible danger. And it underlined Britain's growing air supremacy, bringing devastation to a vital industrial region. But in terms of life the toll was heavy. Of the 19 aircraft with 133 young men who that morning had packed the briefing room at Scampton to hear what their destination would be, only 11 were to return. And from the eight bombers which were lost only three men survived.

Flt Sgt John Pulford was among the lucky ones that night and along with the rest of the crew of AJ-G returned to base and the inevitable party. Then followed three days leave and a visit to his home in Hull.

Born in 1920 in Lorne Street, as a boy Pulford attended St Paul's School. On completing his education he joined the staff of the Paragon Motor Company on Anlaby Road but when war broke out he left to join the RAF, his apprenticeship uncompleted.

Besides being a supreme achievement gained in the face of the gravest danger the dams raid came at a time of great personal sadness for Flt Sgt Pulford. Shortly before the target was revealed to the bomber crews he had been at home in Hull for the funeral of his father. So vital was he to the mission that police escorted him on his journey home.

He flew with Gibson for some time and besides the dams raid had also taken part in the famous attack on the battleship *Tirpitz*. During his flying career with the RAF Flt Sgt Pulford flew more than 79 hours on operations, completing 11 sorties.

It was in January 1944 when tragedy struck. During a raid the aircraft in which he was flying came in to land, tried to take off again and crashed on a hillside. He was 24 years old. And on that day he should never have flown at all, but had volunteered to take the place of another man.

It was not only the men who flew with the RAF who earned honour – and medals – for their efforts in World War Two. Ordinary people were also rewarded for acts of bravery. Among them were two Hull skippers, a housewife, and a Hull boy serving as a messenger in his devastated city. Their stories are here among the tales of Forces bravery...

The Nazi raider who decided to shoot up a Hull trawler did not reckon on the courage of Skipper Frederick Kirby. With five crewmen injured as a result of a bomb dropped by the Focke Wulf as the vessel fished in the North Atlantic, Skipper Kirby decided it was time for action. Twice the aircraft dropped bombs and machine-gunned the trawler. Then it lined up for the 'kill'.

And that's when Skipper Kirby decided enough was enough. He raced to the Lewis gun, held his fire until the last possible moment – and let the Nazi have it, forcing the plane to break off its attack. For his courage Skipper Kirby was awarded the MBE.

Talking of the incident he said: 'Jerry won the first round. We were well ahead on points on the second round. I won the third round and he threw in the towel in the fourth.'

Skipper Kirby, who received an ankle and calf injury when hit by shrapnel, said:

> *Picking up our gun I handed it to a Frenchman on board our vessel to replace the pan with a new one full of ammunition, telling the crew to keep under cover and at the same time to keep an eye on me lest I got a packet and then one of them could jump to it and take charge of the gun.*
>
> *Keeping behind the starboard trawl door for a shield and helped by the steam from the winch (a steam pipe had been hit by a bullet), I sat and waited and as soon as he got into line, I let him have the full pan of ammunition.*
>
> *If one bullet missed him he was lucky. He did not fly over us again, but zoomed away over the ship's stern. As we watched to see whether he was coming back again, smoke suddenly belched from him and he turned in the opposite direction making a wide circle.*

A short time later the mate reported that the aircraft was sitting on the water some distance from the trawler. 'By the time I got on the bridge all I could see was a little bit of something disappearing,' said Skipper Kirby.

The gun fighter

The Germans came up against tough opposition when they came face to face with Harry Duffin, a Hull trawler skipper who enjoyed nothing more than reading novels about the gunslingers of the Wild West. Harry, it turned out, was something of a gun fighter himself and it was to earn him an MBE.

The Nazis chose to attack his trawler seven times. And every time they came up against strong opposition with the gun on the vessel roaring defiance.

On one occasion a German aircraft made several dives in an attempt to bomb the vessel, and tried to rake her decks with gunfire. But each time Harry, who was 52 years old at the time, was on the bridge to direct operations. In the end his efforts were successful – the German gave up.

In another incident enemy aircraft swooped in time after time, hitting one of the trawlers in the 'pack'. Its crew were thrown into the sea. Skipper Duffin managed to get his vessel to the men despite a fusillade of machine-gun bullets which rained down from the planes. But every man was saved thanks to his efforts.

A citation which came with his MBE said: 'He has always succeeded in beating off the enemy, due in no small measure to his courage and determination.'

Courage of a farmer's wife

Danger in the skies as he desperately tried to avoid the three Hurricane fighters which eventually shot him down was only part of the terror faced by a young German airman on hot July day in 1940. For after parachuting to safety he came to face with... Mrs Norma Cardwell.

The Nazi, who had been on a bombing mission, had no stomach left for a fight and Mrs Cardwell, of East Carlton near Aldbrough, had no weapon to defend herself. But her courage in arresting the Nazi flyer brought her the MBE.

And it even drew praise from Prime Minister Winston Churchill, who said the propaganda of her capture was worth a flotilla of destroyers. Mrs Cardwell had the honour of receiving her award from King George VI and Queen Elizabeth, who went personally to present it to her at Hornsea.

She told reporters her version of one of the most remarkable captures of the war. It all began when a farm boy rushed to her door shouting 'German parachutists are coming!' A glance out of the window confirmed the fact and she saw the parachute dropping slowly to the earth.

'I dashed upstairs to look for my husband's gun and then wondered whether it would be the wisest thing to take it,' she said. 'I hesitated and then decided it would not, for the German might have been a better shot than myself.'

As the German landed she marched towards him. 'When I got near him I put on my fiercest frown and looked as stern as I could.

'I felt small beside the airman, but I could see he was terrified. He looked green. I ordered him to hold up his hands, but he didn't understand what I meant. I put up one of my hands to show him. Then he put both hands up.

'I walked nearer to him and put my hands on his revolver and said "Give me this".'

Mrs Cardwell waited with the man by the roadside until a soldier arrived on a motorcycle. He was followed by others who marched the German away. Later two more crewmen from the aircraft were arrested.

Brave Mrs Cardwell said she did not feel afraid during the incident. 'The German didn't understand any English. He only smiled once and that was when I made signs that I wanted a souvenir,' she said.

A pilot's courage

Wounded and bleeding badly a Cottingham pilot flew his bomber home to safety – thanks to the help of a crew member. As Sgt Pilot Jack Henson battled to bring the Blenheim back from France the flow of blood from the severed vein in his neck was staunched by the plane's observer, who stuck his thumb across the wounds.

The drama followed a daylight raid on Merville aerodrome. But the Germans soon struck back and Messerschmitt fighters swept into the attack, pouring wave after wave of cannon fire into the bombers.

A splinter embedded itself in Sgt Henson's neck and, almost fainting from loss of blood, he battled to bring the aircraft back across the Channel. As he did so the observer, Sgt Colman, moved near the pilot and staunched the flow of blood by pressing his thumb against the wound.

Slowly the Blenheim began to recover from the attack, but then a second wave of 10 fighters raced in sensing a quick and easy kill. Gunners managed to account for two of them and despite his injury Sgt Henson managed to manoeuvre the aircraft away from the pack. Running low on fuel by now the fighters turned and headed for home, the Blenheim limping over the coastline with Sgt Colman still holding his thumb across his pilot's wound.

By now Sgt Henson was very weak indeed, and in a state of near collapse due to loss of blood. The bomber veered off course and collided with a sister aircraft, causing it to turn over. But slowly the pilot managed to right the aircraft and keep it with the formation as it limped towards the coast of England.

Still weakening Sgt Henson urged his crew to bail out, fearing that he would be unable to land the plane. But they stayed on board, managing to persuade him to attempt to take her down. Slowly the plane limped towards its base and relief flooded through its crew as the runway came into sight. But more drama was yet to come.

As he approached and made ready to land Sgt Henson tried to put the flaps down only to find the aircraft going into a spin, one of the ailerons having been shot away by the fighters. With a supreme effort he managed to pull the giant aircraft level and eventually land it safely.

It was a heroic action which brought him not only the gratitude of his fellow crewmen, but also the Distinguished Flying Medal for what was described as 'a remarkable feat of endurance, determination and courage'.

After a spell in hospital Sgt Henson recovered from his injury and took to the air again. But six months later after that heroic flight home he did not return from a bombing raid.

Boy became a hero

As Hull burned from wave after wave of Nazi bombing raids 17-year-old James Hodgson became a hero. Yet he should never have been anywhere near the incident which earned him not only the highest praise but also the British Empire Medal.

It was 1941 and Hull reeled from the attacks which turned the city centre into rubble and homes throughout the area into smouldering ruins. James worked with the AFS in Hull as a full-time messenger and on the night of his greatest adventure he should not have been on duty at all – he was officially on holiday.

As the bombs started to fall James, who lived in Lister Street, decided that he should be out there, ready to lend a hand if possible. His story was later told to the *Hull Daily Mail*:

> First of all I put out some incendiary bombs and then went to a wrecked house under which I heard that a number of people were trapped.
>
> A tunnel was being made under the wreckage and I volunteered to crawl through it. At the end of the tunnel I could see Beatrice Dove, a 15-year-old girl who used to go to the same school as myself and who lived in the same street.
>
> She was pinned under the debris with only her face and a hand showing. She was laid on a couch with a dead three-year-old child alongside her and her dead father laid over her.

Below this wreckage was a blazing inferno, so hot in fact that I had to take a stirrup pump to cool the bricks and the other wreckage around Beatrice.

She was crying out for water, so I fed her through a baby's bottle.

The girl complained about pains in her back and James tried to take her mind off it.

I tried to make her forget about her troubles by chatting to her about pictures we had seen at local cinemas.

Have you been to the Regent tonight?' I inquired. 'No I have seen it, I will not be going to the pictures any more after tonight,' she replied.

A few minutes later she was dead, for shortly after I got out of the tunnel the remainder of the premises had collapsed. Ten people were killed, all being smothered.

When James received the award the incident was described as 'one of the finest of youthful heroism in the present war'. But James was not alone in showing the greatest of courage that dreadful night.

Also honoured with the George Medal was Harry Cardwell, of Kingston Gardens, Hull, who at great personal risk had managed to reach the girl and then stayed with her for several hours to comfort her.

Bravery at sea

They were hungry, thirsty and desperate, their dinghy drifting helplessly on hostile seas. For 11 long and tortuous days they fought for survival, being allowed only one mouthful of water a day. But they survived, thanks largely to the efforts of Hull bomber pilot Harold Vertican.

May 1943 saw the Tunisian campaign and Warrant Officer Vertican and his crew airborne and in action. But things went dramatically wrong. First the starboard engine of the Halifax bomber failed. Then the port inner engine went, too. The aircraft was losing height and the crew reacted swiftly, tearing out anything not vital to their flight and throwing it from the plane.

It was a losing battle. The bomber, losing power and battling to keep height against strong winds, was down to just 1,000ft when calamity struck. A third engine failed.

The official citation was later to take up the story: 'WO Vertican was now faced with a perilous situation but skillfully he brought the aircraft safely down on to a rough sea causing no injury to any of his crew, all of whom successfully embarked in the dinghy.'

But as they drifted helplessly about 40 miles off the safety of the coast WO Vertican became increasingly worried about their water supplies. There was only one course of action he could take, and that was to ration it to just one seventh of a pint a day for every man on board.

Cleanliness and activity were also essential in the fight for life and those men who could swim were ordered to take a daily dip in the sea. Those who could not were lowered over the sides.

Eventually relief came and the men were rescued. And on their return to base WO Vertican was ordered to appear before Air Chief Marshall Sir Sholto Douglas to recall his experiences. He was granted an immediate commission on the field, a distinction which was rarely conferred.

But there was more to WO Vertican than that. During the time he was reported missing he received another award for bravery, the Distinguished Flying Cross for his role in an incident which happened in an air attack on Leros.

The citation would say: 'The objective was successfully bombed, but while still over the target area one engine of his aircraft became unserviceable. Despite this he flew the bomber back to base.'

There were, however, problems on the horizon, for fog was blanketing the area and they could not land.

'Undeterred he flew on, searching for another landing ground. The situation became serious and all moveable equipment was jettisoned to assist in maintaining height,' said the citation. 'WO Vertican made a landing after a flight of 700 miles with one of the aircraft's engines out of action.'

Drama in the sky

It was to be just another training flight. In the end it led to a Goole soldier receiving a medal for bravery. The drama unfolded in the skies over North Africa in 1943 when Sgt Instructor Alfred Cook was training soldiers in the art of parachute jumping.

But problems came when one man jumped and his 'chute failed to open, leaving him swinging below the aircraft, hanging on only by his static line. Sgt Cook reacted instantly and desperately tried to haul him back inside the plane, but without success.

This left him only one option. He took a parachute off one of the trainees, put it on and secured himself to the plane before climbing out of it and down the static line which held the trapped man.

High above the ground as the aircraft continued at over 200mph they swung in the air current, until Sgt Cook was able to catch the man's foot with one hand, trying to release his parachute with the other. But the ordeal was not over yet.

The slipstream of the aircraft brought more danger. The men began swinging around as the plane held its speed and height and Sgt Cook's rigging line started to wrap around that of the trapped man.

A report of the incident would later say: 'Sgt Cook, realising that his own parachute was becoming fouled, ordered the man to hold on to him while he dropped in an effort to pull him free to enable both to descend on his own parachute.'

Cook released himself but the other soldier – a Private Trevor – was unable to retain his grip on Cook's harness. Cook landed safely and Trevor was eventually pulled back into the aircraft before it landed.

Later Sgt Cook was awarded the George Medal for what was said to be 'an exceptionally courageous effort.'

Saved by a ghost ship

A derelict torpedoed vessel which meandered on a lonely course across the angry waters of the North Atlantic gave hope and shelter to men who were on the brink of death. Among them was Edward Mouat, of Steynburg Street in Hull, a ship's carpenter who became a hero.

It was January 1941 and on a miserable, bleak evening a torpedo carved across the waters and ripped into the engine room of a cargo vessel, tearing a gaping hole in her side. Within seconds the crew were on deck, racing against time to launch lifeboats, eventually managing to free three of them, each one filled with survivors.

For those on two of the boats there was at least an element of luck. They were picked up within 36 hours. But for the third, with Edward Mouat and 12 others on board, there was no such salvation. Cold, afraid and alone they drifted on and on.

Their plight was desperate, for as they were pulling away from their sinking ship a second torpedo had smashed into its side, creating a tremendous surging wave which damaged the lifeboat, causing water to pour in.

The survivors watched their ship go down and prepared to battle for their lives in a sinking boat which had to be continually baled out with the only equipment to hand – one bucket and a few tins.

Food, too, posed a major problem. Supplies consisted of emergency rations only, among them ships' biscuits, compressed food tablets and chocolate.

Mr Mouat, who had 20 years seagoing experience, found himself in charge of the boat and its navigation and for five long days helped keep the boat afloat. And finally, through the gloom, they saw a ship, and with a supreme effort summoned sufficient energy to make their way towards it. But the seas were huge and they could not approach it too closely for fear of their boat being dashed to piece against its hull. Despite their cries for help there was no response.

Darkness fell. And the lifeboat rode out the night on what the survivors believed was the lee side of the vessel. But in the darkness the ship had vanished.

For two more days they floated helplessly, their hopes of rescue diminishing. But then they saw it again, the mystery ship, looming above them through the grey light of a northern dawn.

By now the survivors were a sorry bunch. One man had died and was buried at sea, the rest were suffering from severe frostbite and exposure. But the ship brought new hope and cautiously, agonisingly, they managed to haul themselves aboard.

An official report of the incident was later to say that the vessel which 'saved' them was in fact derelict, having been torpedoed. Although its bows were low in the water the remainder of the ship was watertight and the survivors found to their delight food, water and clothes left by the crew who, fearing it would sink, had taken to their own lifeboats.

Also left behind was the ship's black cat, which still stalked the vessel. The survivors lived aboard the derelict ship for eight days before being rescued by a British warship.

The efforts of Mr Mouat in helping the men survive were honoured with the award of the British Empire Medal (Civil Division). The citation told of his 'fine qualities of courage and leadership'.

But although the men came through their ordeal there was to be one more casualty. The black cat did not reach safety. Mr Mouat said later: 'She would not come with us. She absolutely refused to leave and when one of us tried to carry her away she scratched, bit and struggled...'

When terrorists came to Hull

Problems with Ireland have faced the British Government for centuries. But as the 20th century began the Fenian movement struck back with a series of terrorist outrages across the country. Among places where terrorists were based was Hull – in the area now occupied by the city's bus station.

A telegram started the scare. It arrived at Hull's main police station in Parliament Street from the force in Newcastle and contained a request for Hull constables to meet a train which was due to arrive at Paragon Station at about midnight.

The Hull bobbies were asked to watch out for and then to 'shadow' a notorious Fenian organiser called Captain Phelan. The mission began well, the Irishman being easily recognised from the description provided. He was tracked to the Salisbury Hotel in George Street, but the authorities had no definite charge which they could bring against him and all they could do was to keep an eye on his movements around the town.

For hours they maintained a patient vigil from a furniture shop across the street. Phelan moved about freely, mixing with people who were thought to be sympathetic to the Irish cause, but he never gave anyone any cause whatever for complaint.

Shortly before his arrival in Hull, however, the police had received a warrant for the arrest of another Irishman called Kearney, who was believed to have taken part in an outrage in Glasgow where the city's gasworks were blown up. Hull police were led to believe that he was living in Collier Street, but despite lengthy inquiries no trace could be found.

One day, however, Phelan sauntered as far as the Haworth Arms and there met a man with one arm. That man was Kearney. The police maintained a constant watch, following both men back to the town and seeing them part company in Brook Street. Kearney went to the address they had been given in Collier Street and Phelan headed towards his hotel.

That evening the police swooped on Collier Street in force and surrounded the building, only to find that the Irishman had received a tip-off and had left, dressed, it was believed, as an old woman.

By now Phelan knew he was under constant surveillance and decided to take the bull by the horns, marching into the police station and demanding to see the officer in charge, saying he would not leave until he saw the Chief Constable in person.

Eventually the chief agreed and while he talked with the Irishman other officers despatched a telegram to the Home Secretary in London asking if they should detain him. The answer was a firm 'no'.

The Irishman was no fool and realised he was being kept talking to detain him as long as possible. He became increasingly annoyed with the Chief Constable, produced a pistol saying he would shoot the first officer who touched him, then backed towards the door and ran, vanishing into the night. Despite a frantic – and wide – search the police found no further trace of him and it was assumed he had left the country.

The Salisbury Hotel later changed its name to the Manchester and later New Manchester Hotel.

The reluctant sailor

Without doubt the town of Howden was a pleasant place in which to live.

It was small, yet interesting, boasting, as one writer would later record, some well-built houses. It was also a town with a long and colourful history, the earliest mention of it being in a charter dating back to the year 959.

One of those who found Howden to his liking was Daniel Defoe, who called there as part of his *Tour Through The Whole of Great Britain* in 1708. He found it 'subject to the inundations from the river [Ouse] occasioned by the freshes which come down from the Wolds; and has been so, it seems, since 1390, when the Bishop of Durham built a very tall steeple to the church, that in the case of sudden inundation, the people might save themselves'.

Not a lot happened in Howden, except on a handful of special occasions which seemed to dominate the local calendar, but the town was, nevertheless, quite lively for a small community with a weekly Saturday market.

An annual wool market which attracted widespread interest was held there each June. And then there was the annual horse fair held in September on the first Monday after the Doncaster races.

This event was eagerly awaited, and always had been, since it was first held under the terms of a charter granted by King John in 1200. The following centuries had seen it grow in size until it clearly justified the proud claim of Howden people to being the largest of its kind anywhere in the country, visited by dealers not only from all over England, but from the Continent too.

During the fair the town took on a most animated appearance. As regards horses, the different hotels and inn yards were filled to overflowing, a great many beasts being without stalls. It was an event to savour – and the townsfolk certainly did that.

It was during the fair in the early years of the 19th century, when they listened to the variety of accents and rubbed shoulders with the hundreds of visitors who flocked to Howden for that special event, that two young men first began to talk of the decision that would change their lives. One of them was Robert Gibson, who came from an old established Howden family. His friend, John Arundel, with whom he had first become acquainted during childhood, also came from a respected family in the town.

Like many young men locked into the boredom of life in the countryside, facing prospects that held out little in the way of dramatic change, they would often talk of their lives and what the future held in store. Howden offered little in the way of opportunity and excitement. But Hull, or so they were led to believe by travellers who passed through, offered the promise of a very different life.

Deciding to make a move did not take long for two youngsters with the lust for adventure and a new way of life and after tearful farewells to their families and firm promises to return as soon as they began to establish themselves in their new home they set off on foot carrying their worldly possessions in bags made by their mothers.

Hull was not a town of imposing architecture. Nor was it a place where the unwary were likely to survive for long. But the scale of the place, the packed streets of the central area, overwhelmed them. Noises assailed them from every quarter, children were everywhere and beggars roamed the streets. From taverns drunken men and women staggered into the ill-paved streets, which were littered with debris and filth. And over the whole town there hung a sweet and sickly smell in the warmth of the spring sunshine.

Yet despite all this there was a feeling of excitement about the place. There was also danger.

Robert Gibson's story

It was as I began to explore an area which I now know to be the High Street that I fell victim to the attentions of Jem White and his friends, the confrontation coming shortly after we had managed to find cheap lodgings in a rather unpleasant little terrace which ran from Blackfriargate. Naturally inquisitive and more than a little excited, I could not wait to explore further. John was not so keen to do so, being of slighter build than myself and more easily tired following our long hike.

At first I did not appreciate that the shouts behind me were in fact directed at me. It was only when I found myself surrounded by a number of aggressive, badly dressed men carrying an assortment of weapons ranging from clubs to cutlasses, that it first occurred to me just what danger I was in.

They acted swiftly and without mercy despite my protestations, binding my arms behind me with thick and coarse rope and marching me through the crowded streets to a boat moored in the harbour. Women shouted abuse at the men when they saw my plight, but to no effect – the men who had seized me simply cursing them and occasionally lashing out with weapon or a boot in an attempt to silence them.

It was not until I was aboard the tender moored in the Hull Roads and met other fellow victims of the gang that I realised just what my fate was. The following day we were transferred to a man o' war. It was the beginning of enforced service with the Navy which was to be my life for almost half a century.

Back in Hull, John, so I learned five decades later, searched for days in a vain bid to find me, but obviously without success. My fate was that of many others in Hull, for White and his gang were all-powerful and no man dared stand against them…

Jem White. The name struck terror into the citizens of Hull. And among them were those who believed – often wrongly – that they were his friends. Like his father Jackey before him, White was the most hated man in town, a tall, tough, thick-set thug who was mean, violent and nasty, a vicious bully who as a leading member of the Press Gang roamed the streets and taverns efficiently and ruthlessly carrying out the will of no less an authority than Parliament itself. It was a role in which he took pride and one which gave him the dubious aura of respectability to cover his tracks.

Although White's reputation was widely known to the residents of Hull visitors to the town would travel in ignorance. All too often it was to prove their downfall.

But such was the hatred of his fellow citizens for White that it was not long before he was being sought by angry citizens, appalled at what he did. Matters came to a head when a mob hell-bent on revenge for his deeds took the law into their own hands. The gang was led by women whose men had been forced into the Navy.

The whole affair moved towards its climax when a wild and unruly mob marched down West Street to White's house where they halted, baying and screaming for his blood.

But nasty as he was, no one doubted his courage, and he showed it to the full on this particular occasion, facing up to the group, who were by now throwing stones as well as abuse, with a cutlass in his hand.

And so the stand-off remained until, as one old record tells us: 'A strong body of soldiers from the main guard in Waterworks Street arrived, dispersed the crowd and took him to the tender, the women following him and calling him names.'

This was but one incident during the years of the Press Gang, which was widely reviled and feared in Hull, a terror which built up to such proportions that it eventually ended in riots.

In the Humber, moored just off the Hull Garrison, was the warship known as *The Inner Guard*. From time to time another vessel, appropriately known as *The Outer Guard*, was seen further down river. The Press Gang, comprising two officers and 12 men, did its work for the King on shore, prowling the streets and public houses day and night seizing any reluctant sailor they could lay their hands on.

But it was not all plain sailing, as the events of July 1774 were to show. A whaler called the *Sarah and Elizabeth* was sailing home to Hull that month from the Davis Straits when she was attacked by the Royal Navy frigate *Aurora* with the intention of pressing the crew.

Fearful of what was happening the crew took refuge below the hatches, in what was to prove a futile attempt to avoid the might of the Navy. The marines aboard the *Aurora* were not men to be messed with and opened fire, killing one man and wounding three others.

After that it was easy – the crew were carried away to Navy service while 15 men from the frigate took the whaler back to Hull. On shore, however, the word spread quickly and the bubbling resentment against 'pressing' built up to crisis proportions. At the coroner's court a jury decided that the dead man had been willfully murdered and Mr Pease, a local banker, went to London demanding an investigation. He was to some extent successful in achieving justice, since the frigate's captain was removed, put aboard a 74-gun ship and packed off to the East Indies for several years.

But still pressing went on, with more and more men being taken against their will and sent to sea, actions which brought simmering unrest from the local population. Typical

Four views of the streets of old Hull.

of the reaction to the work of White and his men was that of a group of women in the Newland area.

They were well aware of the reputation of the Bull Inn on Beverley Road in Hull, which was a popular haunt with members of the Press Gang, who would lie in wait for passing coaches and seize any sailors who happened to be passengers.

According to a local historian: 'On one occasion they stopped a coach and dragged from it a sailor who struggled violently with his kidnappers. A number of women who were haymaking in the neighbouring field came to the rescue and with their hay forks put the gang to flight. These brave Amazonians then placed the sailor in a carrier's wagon, shouldered their hay forks and escorted him through Newland Bar.'

Among working men, too, there were acts of defiance and bravery. One incident in particular attracted not only public comment, but also widespread support from local people. It involved men working in one of the Hull shipyards. Their shift over, they made towards the local taverns before heading for home at the end of what had been just another typical working day. Until, that is, one of them was 'jumped' by members of the Press Gang.

Historian James Sheahan takes up the story:

A regular fight took place and the assailed man jumped into the Humber Dock hoping to effect his escape by swimming.

Immediately two of the human bloodhounds took to the water after him and the strife that followed was terrific. The ship-wright seized one of the gangs-men by the throat and held him with an iron grip; the other gangs-man beating his antagonist over the head with one hand and furiously striking the water with the other. During this time a furious fight was going on between the gang and the ship-wrights on the dockside. The battle in the water was terrible, each struggling with hate and death.

'At length some sailors from a neighbouring vessel put off in a boat and rescued the intended victim from the gangs-men in a very exhausted state.

By 1778 resentment was building up that would finally explode into violence on the streets. It happened when the whaling ship *Blenheim* was returning to Hull from Greenland from a trip which had been both long and hard. But as they busied themselves in preparation for their homecoming the crew reckoned without meeting up with the men-of-war *Nonsuch* and *Redoubt* who, on sighting the whaler, quickly dispatched boats to press the fishermen into Navy service.

But it was to prove much more difficult than either captain believed, for the men of the *Blenheim* were made of sterner stuff and fought off the Navy with knives and spars which were used in whaling operations. The fierce fight was loud enough to attract the attention of the *Nautilus*, a sloop which was moored in Hull Roads and which sent out a boat of its own to lend the Navy men a hand.

The crew of the whaler, determined they were not going to be rounded up, confined their captain and the pilot to a cabin and took the ship over, driving her towards the harbour, where she ran aground at the entrance. The Navy now sensed that victory was in sight and boats from the warships surrounded the *Blenheim* and tried to board her.

In the mêlée shots were fired but the Navy came off worse, with several men being 'desperately wounded'. Two later died in hospital. As for the *Blenheim*, none of her crew were injured, all managed to get ashore and no one was 'pressed' into the King's service, much to the delight of the huge crowds which packed the shipyards in Humber Street and Garrison Side to watch the amazing scenes.

The unlucky captain of the *Blenheim* who missed the action thanks to the decision of his crew to impound him was to find himself in real trouble when he came ashore, being arrested and taken to York where he was charged with the murder of Royal Navy personnel. But the court acquitted him and he was able to return to Hull to a hero's welcome, being chaired through the town by cheering crowds.

Just what happened to White and his gang appears to have gone unrecorded.

Many years after White and his gang had vanished from the scene the final act in the story of Robert Gibson and John Arundel was still to be played out...

Robert Gibson's story

My years at sea were finally over. I returned to England and to Hull to try to build a new life in my remaining years.

Times and conditions had changed. Life was generally improved. But adapting to conditions ashore after a career in the Navy to which I had been sentenced for so many years was difficult.

I had tried to escape from the service of the country, making a lone and desperate bid for my freedom when we had docked in Portsmouth in the Forties, but without success. They had quickly caught me as I tried to hide and taken me back to throw me into prison. It was an experience which I would not wish to relive.

I had served in the Navy against my will until England and France ended their war. It was not a good existence for the men of the Navy were of the worst kind and the morals of those of every rank was of the lowest order. Throughout the years I tried hard to preserve my faith and my dignity, my efforts resulting in my ill-founded attempt to escape what was little more than a life sentence.

And so I, a man who until he came to Hull had never even seen the sea, spent the best part of his life sailing it, eventually being returned to the port where I was captured after decades of being ruthlessly forced to live on the scant rewards for service to King and country.

In Hull I knew no one but was keen to at least attempt to become a part of the community. With that in mind I joined the Congregation Church in Fish Street. It was there that I met the Revd James Sibree, a kindly and decent man, of whom years later a newspaper was to write: 'no man was better known'.

It was while attending a meeting of the Hull Auxiliary of the London Missionary Society that my faith in both God and human nature was at last restored. The speaker had come from London especially for the occasion and the church was packed to capacity to hear his words.

When I saw him the years sped by and I realised that here in this same building was the man I had last seen when I left him in a cheap lodging house to explore the streets of Hull.

By staying in our room John Arundel escaped the attentions of the Press Gang and soon became integrated into Hull life, joining the Fish Street Congregational Church and eventually becoming pastor of the church based at Whitby.

But his travels were not over, and his next appointment saw him in London, where he was appointed minister in charge of Southwark and was secretary of the London Missionary Society. And it was in the latter role that he eventually found his way back to Hull.

And so pensioner met preacher, now the both of us old and grey-headed. We smiled as we shook hands, and then embraced, tears now coursing down our cheeks.

That was how it ended. For years we continued to keep in touch, still friends, both having lived very different lives. How many other victims of the Press Gang I wonder eventually managed to find themselves at peace with their fellows?

Author's note: The story of what happened to Robert Gibson and John Arundel is true. For the sake of the narrative it has been necessary to use first person material as if from Robert Gibson. This does not exist. However, all factual material attributed to him is taken from published records.

Guilty or not?

For Constable Johnston it was an ordinary beginning to another ordinary working day. Eleven o'clock on a bright, but chilly, March morning saw him, as usual, on his beat in Paragon Street. It was not a role he relished.

Johnston knew his patch well, having walked the mean streets of the town for well over 10 years, but in all that time he had never come to terms with what went on in Paragon Street, described by one local journalist in a hard-hitting article on the state of law and morality in the town as 'an offence in the eyes of all decent minded people'.

The morning saw Paragon Street slowly coming to terms with what had gone on the night before. Already many of its inhabitants were sipping their first drinks of the day. By early afternoon they would be spoiling for trouble with drunken brawls commonplace along the whole stretch of the street.

There was, however, mounting sympathy for the lot of PC Johnston and the other members of the hard-pressed force who faced similar problems across the town. Richard Cooke was the owner and editor of the *Hull Critic*, a weekly newspaper which took a satirical and also a serious look at life. Cooke was no stranger to controversy, nor was he a man to mince his words: 'I do not envy the poor policeman who has Paragon Street for his beat. He has to exercise the utmost forbearance, good temper and tact while at the same time he is powerless to compel those who offend public decency to retire to their homes...'

It was not only what went on along the streets which was causing problems. There were major difficulties with what happened at all hours of day and night behind closed and battened doors across Hull. According to Cooke: 'One of the first acts of a new home secretary should be to bring in a bill which would give the police the power subject to a case being proved to the satisfaction of the magistrates so that all well-known houses of ill-fame could be instantly closed and the residents evicted.'

Like PC Johnston, Mr Campbell, the Chief Constable, was well aware of the problems, but knew that keen though he was to crack down on crime in the town, in some cases he was powerless to take effective action. Brothels existed because landlords allowed them to. But generally the chief's no-nonsense stand had proved popular. The effects of tougher policing were most certainly being felt by the criminal community.

The chief had not been in the job for very long, having been picked from a short list of six to head a police force with immense problems of its own after Thomas Cooke, his predecessor, had been asked to leave. Until the appointment of a successor the role of chief had been filled by members of the Watch Committee and in particular its chairman, Mr Stuart.

It had proved an ineffective arrangement, one which prompted one newspaper to comment: 'It is painful at every meeting [of the Watch Committee] to sit and listen to the petty disputes and the trumpery offences with which policemen are charged and it would be amusing, if it were not disgusting, to see the way the chairman and the committee examine and cross-examine the poor delinquents who are brought before them. It is to be hoped that when the new chief is appointed, he will be allowed to manage his own men and be something more than a chief constable in name.'

What was needed was a man who was upright, honest and determined to enforce the law in the interests of the local citizens. In Mr Campbell, formerly a superintendent with the North East Railway Company in York, Hull probably had such a man. Or so it was believed. Certainly no one would later argue that he had not done his job quite effect-ively. It was the claim made against him that led to problems and to his eventual depar-ture. But the question of whether he was really guilty is still, a century on, in some doubt.

At the time brothels such as those which infested the Paragon Street area abounded throughout the rest of the town too, prompting Cooke to write: 'There are dens in which vice flourishes uninterfered with, where the broadcloth of the pastor and his words of admonition and entreaty are never seen or heard.'

Among them were houses in Queen Street where one 'showed perhaps less poverty than aversion for cleanliness'. Cooke piously continued: 'Before the fireplace is a filthy old hag who for a great number of years has lived on the destruction of the virtue of young girls... but what is the most pitiable sight of all is a young child, a girl of about 11 or 12 years, who unless she is soon to be rescued from the atmosphere of corruption will in all probability sink as deeply into the mire of infamy as the adults who offer her.'

In another house the policeman he accompanied found a young woman who only two weeks before had left the Worsley Street Home for Fallen Girls 'seemingly thoroughly repentant and determined to lead a virtuous life'. Cooke concluded: 'We get sickened at the fearful atmosphere which pervades the whole place...'

Nothing, it seemed, had changed for some time. For the police were a law unto themselves with sober constables being hard to find and a Watch Committee which was said to be so petulant that to run a truly efficient force 'would have been a 13th labour of Hercules'. Into this came Mr Campbell, a tough warrior on the side of law and order determined to bring decency to the streets. It was a battle which won him acclaim from many, but one which was to end with him leaving in disgrace.

In the mid-1880s the fate of the women who were on offer in the dens of vice was causing growing concern and it was a Poor Law guardian and member of the Watch Committee who decided to take the matter up and press for the police to tighten the screws and prosecute brothel keepers under the Criminal Law Amendment Act of 1885. In particular this worthy gentleman wanted to stop the wave of juvenile prostitution.

December of that year saw revelations that despite efforts to cut down on young prostitutes their clients were not always from what was at the time referred to as 'the lower orders'.

But despite the moral protestations about prostitutes and the undoubted determination of the Chief Constable and the Watch Committee to do something about them, other problems began to appear on the horizon.

Edith Creighton was not a prostitute. She was a respectable girl of 14 of poor, but not dishonest, parents. And she may also have had charms which some people, among them the Chief Constable, may have found difficult to ignore.

It had happened, or so it was claimed, when her father was away at sea. Her mother was at work and afterwards attended a meeting of teetotallers. And Edith found herself alone at home with the Chief Constable, himself the father of nine children.

Just why he had called at the house must remain a matter of speculation. And why he decided to stay when neither of Edith's parents were in the house gives food for thought. But stay it seems he did. And wrecked a promising career.

It was alleged that Mr Campbell arrived at the house, in St Thomas's Place, Portland Street, ostensibly to obtain important information. He was said to have asked if anyone could see in, sat down and encouraged Edith to sit on his knee, kissed her and started to unbutton his trousers.

But then, and according to the more charitable, realising the error of his ways, he was alleged to have given the girl sixpence and asked her not to mention what had happened to her mother, a request she did not agree to.

When the matter came before a disciplinary hearing it was said that Mr Campbell, himself the father of nine, had been a regular visitor to the house but all in the line of duty, calling to see Edith's father on what he described as confidential police business.

Cooke took up the story: 'It must be conceded that for a man in middle life to take a full grown girl of 14 upon his knees and fondle her as if she were a two-year-old baby is grossly improper and indiscreet.'

The Watch Committee shared this view and despite hearing Mr Campbell's spirited defence asked their chief to resign, which he eventually agreed to do, but only after pointing out that he had no money at all and requesting three month's salary, which was granted.

Cooke took a high moral tone in the *Hull Critic,* which thundered: 'A chief constable, like the proverbial spouse of Caesar, not only should be, but must be above suspicion and whatever indiscretions may be tolerated in an inferior officer there can be no condonement or excuse for the shortcomings of the head of the force.'

In fact things had not been going too well with the police anyway, a serious complaint regarding its management being made by Mr Justice Hawkins, which prompted Cooke to comment: 'It is possible that some persons may look upon the incident as a lucky termination to an unfortunate appointment.'

Cooke's final word on the affair was more conciliatory. He wrote: 'The Creightons have had satisfaction. Mr Campbell is a disgraced and ruined man, for whatever he did, be it simply an indiscretion or something worse, he has paid dearly and suffered bitterly and the sooner the matter passes into oblivion the better. Meanwhile, every disreputable character in the town is rejoicing greatly over Mr Campbell's downfall, for he was in sooth a terror to evildoers.'

But just how guilty Campbell really was remained a matter of some conjecture. Much of what was being said centred on the girl's parents and whether her story was as incriminating as may have been supposed. As speculation continued friends and sympathisers of the Campbell family started a collection on their behalf, bringing the comment: 'The punishment of the late chief is almost more than he can bear, especially as he is conscious of his own innocence… The facts have transpired which show that the family of the girl are by no means so perfect and angelic as the Watch Committee believed them to be.'

Cooke now declared: 'Mr Campbell may have been perfectly innocent of any felonious intent, part of the girl's story to some may appear to be grossly exaggerated and those who think so would do well, in a private way, to do something which will mitigate the terrible distress into which his unoffending wife and innocent children have been so suddenly plunged. With them, the public, we know, will have the profoundest sympathy.'

'Orrible murder!

Considering it was to be his last night alive Arthur Richardson slept well, as if unaware of what the morning would bring. He awakened at 5am and as the realisation of what was to happen gripped him he was aware of the sound of voices in the corridor outside his cell as men made their final preparations for his execution.

Richardson, a small man who had seen service with the British Army in India, appeared calm to those who saw him in his final hours. He managed to enjoy a hearty breakfast at six o'clock despite the knowledge that he had just two hours left to live.

Among his visitors was the acting prison chaplain, the Revd M. Parkin, Richardson receiving his ministrations most devoutly before taking his last Holy Communion.

It was shortly before eight when William Billington, his hangman, arrived. They had first met the previous evening, Billington visiting the

Arthur Richardson, the first man to be hanged in Hull's Hedon Road Jail.

condemned man to form an idea of how high the drop should be. Because Richardson, who had been found guilty of the brutal murder of his aunt, was of slight build he was given a longer rope than would have been allowed a stouter person.

As Billington entered the cell Richardson quietly rose, allowing his arms to be pionioned. Then, according to one account of the proceedings: 'The painful procession

Offenders in Hull would find themselves locked up in this building, the Old Jail Guard House which stood in Market Place. This is how it looked in round 1780.

commenced and the man who had to pay the penalty of his crime walked calmly, firmly and collectedly along the short path that separated cell from scaffold.

'When on the scaffold he stood erect, whilst his legs were being pinioned. Then the rope was affixed, the cap drawn over his head and the bolt pulled all in a few seconds. Richardson disappeared and the rope merely gave a twitch, death apparently being *instantaneous. The whole proceedings from leaving the cells to the execution occupied a little under a minute...'*

That carefully supervised execution in the Hull Gaol on Hedon Road was the first to be held in the prison. It happened on 25 March 1902, just four months after the crime was committed in what one report would describe as 'the blackest year in Hull's criminal history,' one which saw four murders and one case of manslaughter, a record not shared by any city of similar size.

The gallows on which Arthur Richardson died were not built for him, but for 21-year-old John Aaron Walker, who murdered his father in Raywell Street, Hull, but who was reprieved because of his youth. Until then prisoners sentenced to death had been hanged at York Castle or Armley Gaol. When the castle was converted into a military prison a decision was made to use Hull for capital sentences.

Indeed, some time had passed in the town between hangings. Before Richardson met his fate the last time anyone was hanged in Hull was as far back as 19 August 1778, when John Rogerson was taken by a type of sledge to the gallows which then existed in Thornton Street – the last man to be publicly killed in Hull. Rogerson paid the ultimate price and gained a small place in the history of Hull for counterfeiting.

An eyewitness account of the execution was written by the Revd George Lambert, the first minister of Fish Street Chapel, who spent time with Rogerson as he awaited death and told of 'the awful moment when he was to leave his gloomy mansion...'

His account continued: '...When we came to the fatal tree he evidenced the most unshaken firmness. He then spoke to the people and told them it was an affecting scene which was now before them – a young man but 25 years of age to be launched into eternity. He also warned them against idleness, lying and bad company.' Then came the final moment: 'He stood praying for some time, frequently signifying his desire to be gone by putting one foot down from the place on which he stood. 'At last it was drawn away and he was sent from our world accompanied either with a general groan or a cry for mercy from numerous spectators.'

Forging coins cost several criminals their lives over the years.

At York on 27 March 1575 Frederick Gottfried, a native of Hull, was hanged for the offence. And on 1 August 1639 Robert Skelton, of Hull, was hanged for forging a will belonging to a Mr Thomas Bell who also lived in the town. In 1768 Joseph Hall, a 27-year-old Hull man, suffered death on the gallows at York for coining.

Rebellion was also said to be 'checked by the gallows' in times gone by.

At the York Lent Assizes in 1639 14 men suffered death for the offence and two of them were from Hull – Henry Cave and William Cropper. At the same time a remarkable case from Pocklington was also tried. Isabella Billington, who was 32 years old, was found guilty of crucifying her mother on 5 January 1649 and offering a calf and a cock as a burnt sacrifice. She was found guilty and hanged. So was her husband, who was also involved in the crime.

A crime of a very different kind cost Nathaniel Picket, of Hull, his life in 1684. He faced a court at York for scuttling a ship called *Ararinal* which was lying in the Humber.

Law breakers of the past could expect to face very rough justice. Crimes which today merit little more than community service

The entrance to the old House of Correction which was in Fetter Lane, off Hull Market Place. The building had three storeys and was said to be used as a lock-up 'for the bloods of the town, who, having been more festive than discreet, were here accommodated for the night...'

orders were dealt with severely. Typical was the case of William Riley, of Hull, who robbed John Borr on the highway at Newland in 1785. The punishment – death on the gallows at York. Another Riley – John – met his untimely end on the York gallows in 1859 for the murder of his wife in Hull.

In centuries past the Quarter Sessions in Hull held the power of life or death over those who appeared before them and the judges of the day made the most of those

The first gallows in Hull, shown here in a drawing from the 14th century, were first mentioned in 1299 when King Edward I granted his charter to the town. They are thought to have stood in what is now Jameson Street.

powers. The extent of this is revealed in records dating back to 1527, when Alexander Heynsley, of Gilberdyke, a weaver who also went under the name of Alexander Pringle, received a death sentence at the Quarter Sessions for breaking into All Saints' Church in Hessle. At the same sessions Thomas Hodgson was condemned to death for stealing a white sheep worth 12 shillings at Hessle.

By 1576 Hull was said to be enjoying 'a flood tide of prosperity'. This attracted the attention of pirates, who saw rich pickings in the trade being undertaken to and from the port. According to one historian: 'The Humber's mouth, as well as all the eastern coast, was so harassed and obstructed by them that scarce a merchant ship could still sail with safety. To remedy this evil the Lord High Admiral of England required the town of Hull to fit up two stout ships of war to protect its own vessels, and to assist in scouring the adjacent coast.

'These ships, being well equipped and manned, sailed in quest of the maritime robbers, and they had soon the good fortune to capture several of them and bring them into Hull.'

The pirates were tried by a special commission attended by the Earl of Huntingdon, Lord President of the North. The account added: 'Six of the misguided men were found guilty, and, in virtue of their sentence, were executed and hung in chains at different places on the neighbouring coasts.'

As time passed the death sentence was still used, although, it would seem, on fewer occasions. Judges began, for instance, to take notice of the mental state of the accused.

On 9 January 1872 Priscilla Utting, who was said to have been in an asylum, killed her two-year-old daughter at a house in Hull's Beverley Road workhouse by tying a handkerchief round her neck. She was ordered to be detained at Her Majesty's pleasure.

Jane Crompton, a 65-year-old mother who lived in Osborne Street, managed to escape with penal servitude for life after cutting off her four-year-old daughter's head. The court was told that Crompton disliked the girl and had often wished her dead!

A reprieve saw Robert Searle escape the gallows after a particularly nasty crime in Hull. On 10 January 1875 he was working with James McConnell in the stoke hole of the SS *Sappho*, which was lying in the Albert Dock. The men quarrelled, an argument which was to end with McConnell being stabbed in the chest, receiving wounds which took 40 minutes to kill him. Searle, realising the magnitude of his crime, decided that the only way out was to kill himself, so he cut his

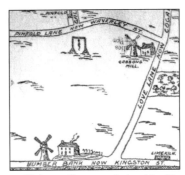

Hull's last gallows are depicted in this 18th-century plan of the town.

own throat. But he didn't do a good enough job, was treated and recovered, and was then sentenced to death. Once again, though, he survived, the following month being granted a reprieve.

Mrs Plant, of 5 Grosvenor Terrace, Grosvenor Street in Hull was not so fortunate when her throat was cut. She was attacked by her husband who then committed suicide by hanging himself.

A strange killing occurred in Hull on 22 December 1883 when Charles Nowland, a pattern maker of 11 Granville Terrace, Strickland Street, threw an iron spittoon at his wife. It caught her on the head and she died from the injury six days later. Nowland was sentenced to death, but later reprieved.

Of all the killers whose names haunt the history of Hull, Fred Oswald Dry must rank as one of the more fortunate. Dry, a private in the East Yorkshire Regiment, killed his wife Madge at their home in Marne Street, off Chanterlands Avenue, on 26 April 1917. A few days later he was discharged at the Hull Police Court by Mr Stonehouse, JP. Dry was free – albeit temporarily.

Next, the public prosecutor intervened and he

Hanging high. This was the gibbet which stood on Beverley Gate, Hull in 1537.

was re-arrested, charged once again with murder and taken before the Hull Police Court. As a result he appeared before York Assizes on 10 and 11 July. The jury, however, could not agree on its verdict and Justice Coleridge ordered that the case should stand over until the following assizes.

On 22 November Dry appeared once more, this time being sentenced to death for the killing, although the jury recommended mercy. And mercy was finally shown. Dry was subsequently reprieved.

Jane Allen was a woman of 'the unfortunate class'. And unfortunate she certainly was the day she met William James Bolton. Bolton was a Hull trawler engineer and was separated from his wife when he met Allen, forming a strong affection for her. It proved, however, a stormy relationship, and one which came to a head when she announced she was to marry someone else.

Bolton lost his temper, stabbed her to death and tried to cut his own throat. He failed, was tried for Allen's murder, and was hanged in Hull Prison on 23 December 1902. Although not public affairs, executions attracted huge public interest. This fascinating and graphic account, published that same day, described the drama outside the prison on Hedon Road as the hour approached and Bolton died.

'A shadow seemed to hang over the grey and grim gaol, so suggestive of solidity and strength; yet a certain rugged authority seemed to sit on the still building as the crowd of interested people stared up at its parapets this morning.

'The more eager fringed the gravel path that flanked the arch with its massive gates at which a man in a warder's clothes would anon peep out as if to remind the waiting crowd that the arrangements were proceeding as quickly as possible.

'Several policemen kept the crowd from the portals of the doors, but the early arrivals were quite content to lean against the black hoarding that runs on the opposite side. Above, on the steep siding, men employed on the docks and others were clustered.

'There were unusual signs of life outside the prison soon after eight o'clock; some who were earlier about saw the grey dawn of another day battling for mastery with the fading darkness.

'Gradually the work-a-day world – the same as any other day for most save the wretched culprit about to pay the penalty. The morbid in the crowd imagined the feelings of the man who was clinging to a life which was only a question of minutes. As the minutes dragged miserably by snatches and points of the murder story were re-told and comments made.

'Soon after 8.30 Mr T. Morrill, JP, representing the Hull magistrates, drew up in a dog cart and, stepping briskly down, left his man holding the horse by a bridle, a sure sign that he would soon return... The minutes before nine could not be counted on one hand.

'Women were present in large force; they were chiefly of the poorer class and some were taking an emotional interest in the rapidly approaching awful ceremony.

'Although waited for so long the hour seemed in the end to come with suddenness.

'The same instant two youths strolled by, carrying a small white coffin on their shoulders. It was a singular, though suggestive precursor of the end of the scene inside the jail for the next moment the bell tolled its first note. Whilst it slowly tolled the crowd gradually dispersed to its work but others remained to study the features of those who were present at the death...'

A town's saviour

He was a most unlikely hero. As far as is known he never saw battle or took part in action against an enemy. He did nothing to achieve any civilian award for bravery.

William Warden was Mr Ordinary, a plumber who lived in Hessle. Yet Warden saved more lives than any hero on the battlefield. Thousands benefitted from his efforts, and apart from being given a silver cup with two handles he never received any official recognition. That went to others, some of whom through their own egotistical greed cheated him of his rightful place in the history of Hull.

William Warden helped bring clear, cool, fresh water to the people of the town. It was a remarkable and far-sighted achievement. Historian James Sheahan was later to write: '...The people of Hull owe him [Warden] a great deal of gratitude... People of Hull be grateful to your greatest benefactor.'

Over a century later Edward Gillett and Kenneth MacMahon would comment on his efforts in their book, A History of Hull: *'...Within the context of public health in Victorian Hull he must be numbered among the foremost of the town's benefactors.'*

The Pope frowned as he carefully perused the document handed to him. It was neatly written, carefully worded and sent as a last resort. It came from the mayor of a town called Hull, on the east coast of England.

His Holiness had better things to do than become involved in what was really a localised dispute. But it was one which did appear to require intervention from someone with power and authority, events having led to open warfare in a place far removed from the cloistered halls of Rome. In Hessle, Anlaby and Cottingham the natives were – yet again – becoming restless. And it was all over water.

It had started in 1376 when the mayor and burgesses of the fast growing town of Hull had complained to the King of England that their community had no fresh water, other than that which was brought in every day on boats from Lincolnshire at great cost and considerable effort.

The King was decisive and ordered an easy and, to most people in Hull, quite acceptable solution. The result was that a ditch was dug 'to convey the pure and liquid stream that bubbled up from the springs of Hessle, Anlaby and Cottingham'. It was enough to start a dispute that would rumble on for 20 years. In the villages anger grew quickly and by the spring of 1392 had reached crisis point.

According to one record: 'They banded themselves together in separate bodies over which captains were appointed and armed themselves as well as they could and also bound themselves together by most solemn oath to stand by and support each other, alleging that they entered into this combination for the purpose of avenging themselves upon the people of Hull for cutting up their fields and depriving them of fresh water.'

Under the threat of personal violence more and more people were recruited, the courses of the waterways which supplied Hull were altered and provisions destined for the town were held up. But Hull remained defiant.

It proved a major setback to the villagers and the protesters who had 'vowed destruction' to the town, ransacking houses and plundering its inhabitants' homes, retreated to lick their wounds at Cottingham. When the sheriff arrived the ringleaders were arrested, some of them being executed at York for their wrongdoings. But the protests still continued.

And then Pope John XXII was asked to intervene by the mayor. In a remarkable letter written in Rome on 20 July 1413 he 'reminded those who at the instigation of Satan had endeavoured to ruin the inhabitants of a large and flourishing town by depriving them of water that they must give a strict account of their deeds at the day of judgement...'

It worked. But despite divine interference there would be more disputes involving the villagers. Many official orders and reports would be issued concerning the supply and quality of water. And the development of pumping stations and waterworks which were to prove ineffective and unhygenic would bring hope of a solution before almost four and a half centuries later the problem of water supplies to Hull was finally resolved.

The railway at Hessle was opened on 1 July 1840. It was a boon to the village, if rather uncomfortable for most of its passengers, who could not afford to travel first class. They had to sit in open carriages.

It was a proud occasion, not only for the town, but also for George Hoyle, who took up the appointment of stationmaster. And it brought the name of William Warden to the public attention for the first time.

Warden was an intelligent man with an inquisitive mind. The arrival of the railway intrigued him. And so did the supply of water. The two came together when he took a look at the arrangements which operated at Hessle for use on the locomotives running on the new stretch of line.

Warden went to work, putting forward suggestions that involved deepening the well used to take supplies to the station and installing fixed pumps at Hessle for supplying the engines with water. It was a great success.

Then he turned his mind to weightier matters.

Enough was enough. Members of the General Board of Health discussed at some length the problems created by an epidemic of cholera in Hull. It was an outbreak which caused concern at the highest levels. As a result an officer was despatched to the town to report, the document which he eventually produced concluding that the supply of water was far too small for a growing town and for the health, cleanliness and general sanitary purposes of its people.

Members of the Corporation were aware of this fact, and armed with official evidence started to seriously investigate ways of improving the situation, calling on the help of some of the top experts in the country, and eventually realising that the man who had the answer they sought was living on their doorsteps.

William Warden's story:

It is not my place to attack the views of men of letters who have greater knowledge than I will ever possess, but nevertheless it must be said that the pontifications of those so-called leaders in their particular fields are not necessarily always the answer to a problem.

In 1842 the Water Committee set up in Hull by the Corporation four years earlier approached Mr Thomas Wickstead, an eminent hydraulic engineer based in London, to look at the whole situation concerning the adequacies of the water supply and where better quality and larger quantities of water could be obtained. Tests on springs in the area disappointed him. They could not, he believed, be depended on for more than half a million gallons a day. So convinced was he of his own beliefs that this learned gentleman came up with a solution of his own – to take almost two and a half million gallons each day from the River Hull, a scheme which would cost some £60,000.

It was a controversial suggestion, but members of the Water Committee were in agreement and on 29 April 1844 the foundations were laid for the Stoneferry Waterworks, the first complete supply from them being issued on 24 August the following year. Naturally enough it was cause for celebration with a large assemblage of influential gentlemen dining in the Public Rooms to celebrate completion of the work.

I was doubtful about it, a trepidation which was later proved to be correct when people in the town began to complain against the quality of the tidal river water, said to be both muddy and salty. And when people in Hull began to think seriously about it they then realised that they were drinking water directly from a river which was polluted by the sewage which flowed down towards the Humber from Driffield and Beverley.

It's fair enough to say that dissatisfaction became so acute even though analytical chemists had tried to assure the population that the water was all right to drink, that the Town Council had no alternative but to bring in another expert from London, the highly acclaimed Mr James Simpson, who directed his attention to Spring Head and arrived at the conclusion that the springs could never supply more than one million gallons a day. The Corporation accepted his views. I did not.

Not deterred, this worthy gentleman turned his attention to West Beck at Driffield and spent £1,200 of Hull's money in experiments which I firmly believed were doomed to failure before they even began.

Our City Fathers were by now becoming desperate and in May 1857 directed their own resident engineer to look at the matter. He came up with a suggestion which would have taken an Act of Parliament to bring to fruition. It never saw the light of day.

Throughout all of this I believed that these so called men of expertise had not carried out their duties with enough care. For years the springs of the area had held a fascination for me. I decided that enough was enough and that it was time to put my own views forward, challenging the opinions of the three engineers. I must now admit that my suggestion that as much as five million gallons of pure water could be taken each day from Spring Head was listened to with great scepticism.

In fact it took them two years to consider my ideas worthy of investigation and a special committee was set up to supervise my work.

I am by nature a simple man and conducted my own experiments in a simple manner, creating bores and placing pumps over them, one being 252ft deep and the other 400ft deep. Imagine my satisfaction when, without pumping they produced two million gallons each day.

My efforts began to attract attention. In fact I was even entertained at a banquet in the Vittoria Hotel at which a toast was drunk to the continuing success of the experiment.'

For a good day out Hull people enjoyed nothing more than the idyllic setting of Spring Head. It was the perfect for a day trip by horse and cart and a picnic, within four miles of the town centre, a pleasant rural ride.

The coming of the waterworks provided the first whispers of the winds of change which were later to roar through this picturesque area. First came water, then the railway and the engine sheds which were to dominate the Spring Head skyline.

But those halcyon times of day trips to the area lived on in the memories of many, among them Hull journalist Henry Corlyon, who was later to write:

As to Spring Head I cherish the most pleasurable recollections. It was an ideal scene and none unless inspired by the gift of poesy could adequately describe it. It was enchantingly sylvan.

Apart from the foliage and springs there was the additional attraction of a mansion which I believe was owned by Mr Lightfoot. It had a large lake in which a number of swans gracefully floated.

Spring Head was visited by thousands of persons on holidays. This was before the age of motor cars, cheap railway facilities and frequent Bank Holidays. The people of Hull, both young and old, thoroughly enjoyed themselves. In fact the scene they presented resembled a gigantic picnic. It was not without deep regret that those who had been in the habit of recreating themselves at the spot learned that it was in contemplation to establish waterworks. But it had to be. The town needed a plentiful supply of pure water.

'...Yes, it was a great shame that much of this pleasant area had to be destroyed and certainly I, William Warden, would have been happy if there had been a chance to preserve Springhead in its entirety. But what I did was absolutely necessary as history has since proved...

Once the Town Council realised the potential of my proposal they acted reasonably quickly, erecting a waterworks at Springhead and laying pipes to convey supplies to the works at Stoneferry from where it could be pumped into the town. Work on this part of the scheme began on 27 January 1862 with the Mayor and various officials turning out to commemorate the occasion.'

The waterworks at Springhead – a legacy to William Warden. The buildings were until recently a museum. They are now closed.

At this time Thomas Dale came on to the scene as resident engineer. Dale proved a valuable asset, a man of 'indefatigable energy and industry' who overcame great difficulties with engineering to complete the scheme. By January 1864 all borings and excavations were finished and it was predicted that Spring Head could supply as much as seven millions gallons of pure fresh water a day when the two pumping engines got to work.

The total cost of the scheme was £50,844. In human terms it was a cheap price to pay. Dale was hailed as a saviour, praise being heaped upon him for his work in designing and supervising construction of the waterworks. In April 1865 there was praise of a more practical nature. The Town Council agreed to pay him a gratuity of £300 for his 'extraordinary services' as well as award him a pay rise of £50 a year.

Warden was not so fortunate. The man who instigated the whole thing received words of praise and little more.

One historian was to sum it up: 'Mr Warden accomplished a great undertaking and the people of Hull owe him a great debt of gratitude. With limited means and in the midst of considerable opposition he has procured for the town one of the greatest earthly blessings, an abundant supply of bright, sparkling and refreshing spring water. ... People of Hull, be grateful, be just to your greatest benefactor.'

But fair they were not. Warden was of Scottish ancestry and it was a 'few natives of the land of his ancestors' who decided to honour him. They presented him with a two handled silver cup to mark his achievement.

Forgotten heroes

For the forgotten victims of a dark and sinister chapter in the history of Hull there are no gravestones and no memorials.

Historians have skimmed over their stories. Yet the fate of people who were starved, beaten, robbed and tortured in a city which today prides itself on its dedication to the preservation of human rights goes almost unnoticed.

The crime of the men and women who suffered in the blockhouses and the castle of Hull was only that they believed in their faith – Catholicism.

Today traffic races over the Myton Bridge which spans the River Hull, and along the road to Hedon, passing near the great new attraction known as The Deep and the site of what was once one of three great blockhouses in which the innocent paid a terrible price for their beliefs.

When, in the 16th and 17th century members of the Catholic faith were put to death at the Tyburns of London and York, Hull became notorious, not for killing, but for 'strictness and severity and for the utter discomfort and hardship meted out by its jailers to Catholic prisoners.'

Many died of 'ill-usage' and were later described as 'martyrs for the faith, who, not being publicly executed were soon forgotten.' This is their story...

Life behind the high, plain walls of the palace was normally sedate. Servants carried out their tasks quietly and efficiently. It was neat, tidy and well-maintained.

Hull from the Humber – the scene in 1603. The southern blockhouse is towards the right of the picture. The towers of Holy Trinity and St Mary's Church are clearly visible.

The day the King came the scene was very different. Nervousness hung in the air, and maids, gardeners, and kitchen staff checked, double checked and checked again that everything was perfect.

It was 1 October 1540 and King Henry VIII was arriving in Hull to take up residence at the Suffolk Palace, a vast and sprawling development across an area which today is bordered by Bowlalley Lane, Quay Street, part of Queen's Gardens and Lowgate.

Henry had special interest in the palace, work on which began in 1387, having bought it from Sir William Sidney and ordered both its repair and fortification. And it was, on his arrival in 1540, an impressive pile.

At the entrance was a lofty gateway over which, supported by strong timbers, were two chambers. The gateway led to an open area 30 yards long and six broad, on to which faced a spacious tower three stories high and containing three chambers, each 18ft square. A courtyard covered with large square paving was adorned on each side by beautiful and elegant buildings. A hall built of brick measured an impressive 60ft in length and 40ft in breadth. On the eastern side were pantries with lodging rooms over them and a kitchen which measured 20ft square.

Another great yard, neatly walled, contained an acre of land with fishponds and a dovecote and to the west lay 'a pleasant plot of ground containing two acres of pasture

Hull as seen from the Humber in the early years of the 19th century. The lofty building to the left is the Theatre Royal which opened on 1 May 1810. Street lamps can be seen in the picture and used whale oil for power. The artist had, however, ideas of his own when it came to depicting Holy Trinity Church. The architectural details at no time in the church's history had the appearance shown in the drawing.

enclosed with a brick wall 9ft high'. The palace had its own chapel, dedicated to St Michael the Archangel and in dimension some 20ft in length and over 15ft in breadth.

It was, believed Henry, an impressively attractive place in which to stay. Especially now that it had been fortified prior to his visit. For on his instructions the palace had been improved to become a 'sitidell and a special kepe of the hole town'. Fortifications included a redoubt of three guns in the walls opposite Chapel Lane, one gun inserted into the wall which faced Bishop Lane and another sweeping the main gateway. Other guns defended the walls in other parts.

Safe behind his walls Henry spent some time during his visit looking at the rest of Hull's defences and declared that although satisfied there was a need for more to be built on the east or harbour side of town. He was adamant about the improvements, writing a specific instruction that they must be made 'mighty strong'.

The powers that be in Hull were quick to act on the King's order. On 22 February 1541 the foundations were laid for what were to become the Blockhouses and the Hull Castle.

The buildings were magnificent, a tribute to their designers and to those who nurtured them. But their days were to end in sadness and destruction, their buildings obliterated on the orders of the King.

In Hull the Blackfriary, the Whitefriary and the Carthusian Priory were said to have 'charmed with their quaint architecture the stranger who visited the picturesque old town. Having existed for more than three centuries under different forms, in poverty and in wealth, in mean-ness and magnificence, in misfortune and in success, they finally succumbed to the Royal will. The day came – and that a drear winter day – when their last Mass was sung, their last censer waved, their last congregation bent in wrapt and lowly adoration before the altar there; and doubtless as the last tones of that day's evensong died away in the vaulted roof there were those who lingered in the solemn stillness of the old massive piles, and who, as the lights disappeared one by one, felt that for them there was now a void which could never be filled because their old friaries, with their beautiful services, their frequent means of grace, their hospitality to strangers and their loving care for God's poor had passed away like an early morning dream and were gone for ever...'

They vanished because of the actions of Henry VIII. Like others across the country they were irreplaceable. The King's reforms led to the loss of three religious houses in Hull. One of them, that of the Blessed Virgin of Mount Carmel, was created in 1307 and was said to be 'a stately building extending along the entire south side of Whitefriargate'.

At about the same time the 'lofty and spacious' friary occupied by monks from the Order of St Augustine was established, later becoming 'ornamented with curious gardens and fountains'. Also in Hull was the Carthusian Priory, with its buildings of 'stately magnificence with extensive gardens' and a chapel said to be 'adorned with splendid altars and pictures'.

In the age of suppression of religious belief these fine buildings were confiscated and destroyed. And the remains were put to a very different use, building the blockhouses and castle. The friars who had so lovingly created places of solitude and peace could never have envisaged that the very stones they had used – even in some cases their own grave covers – would form part of the walls and dungeons in which they and people like them would be imprisoned and tortured.

As well as material from the friaries the builders of the blockhouses also used stone from St Mary's Church in Lowgate, which fell in 1518 owing to defective foundations.

Anthony Atkinson was good at what he did – and that meant hurting people. For Atkinson, Hull's customs searcher, was a vicious tyrant who waged a war of hatred against the innocents.

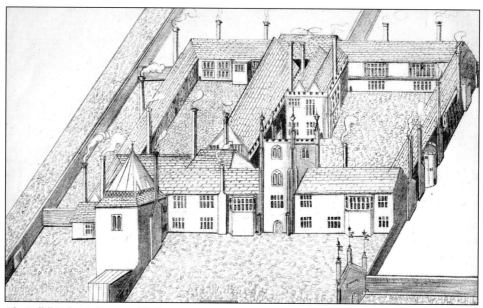

The Suffolk Palace in Lowgate. The late 19th-century writer T. Tindall Wildridge would say of the area covered by the buildings in this drawing: 'The whole area may be said to be nearly surrounded by fine buildings – in Lowgate, the Town Hall, a number of shops and the Hull Exchange; in Bowlalley Lane (on the former bowling green of the palace) a variety of business premises; in Quay Street, various buildings and in the dock side the Hull Dock Company's and other warehouses – but these enclose a girdle of respectability, a district where squalor and misery are the chief features; though it must be confessed that there are instances of health and cleanliness which it is surprising to find in such unpropitious circumstances. Probably the time is not far distant when improved sanitary regulations will cause these crowded courts to give place to a better state of things; when the memory of the old palace will become still more remote, till, unknown on the place of its birth, its only record will be on the historic page.' In fact the palace is today remembered by a plaque on the wall of the former head post office in Alfred Gelder Street. That building is now a housing development.

Atkinson managed to gain his appointment thanks to the influence with members of the Council of the North of a relative, Jane Jobson, of Brantingham. In return for the favour Atkinson paid her £100.

But there was more to Atkinson than watching out for smugglers and cheats. He was also a leading member of a particularly nasty profession – that of priest hunter.

Like members of the Nazi party in occupied Europe 350 years later Atkinson and his kind conducted a hate campaign of such ferocity that it led to ordinary people being imprisoned, tortured and starved to death.

His hatred was total, and was reflected in a letter he wrote to the Earl of Essex and to Sir Robert Cecil: '...There is sundry places in Yorkshire and Lincolnshire that are well known to me and harboureth Joseph Constable and various sundry traitorous priests...'

And then came this: 'In Lincolnshire there is a place called Twigmore and four or five tenements adjoining that harboureth a number of traitorous Jesuits, seminaries and others that are their consorts... the place is one of the worst in Her Majesty's dominions, and is used like a Popish college, for traitors that use the north parts are there harboured.'

Just how dedicated Atkinson was to his task was highlighted by an incident on Christmas Eve 1594 when, at midnight, another priest chaser named Outlaw was sent to search a house. On arrival he met up with Atkinson, who had with him a 'posse' of about 30 men. After smashing their way in they made several arrests, including Father Alexander Rawlings, and all the captives were imprisoned.

One writer was later to say of Atkinson: 'He was a man entirely devoid of character', a fact underlined by what was to happen to him. State papers record that in 1602 Atkinson, with others, got himself in trouble for speaking disrespectfully about a member of the Privy Council. As a result he was sentenced by the Star Chamber to whipping, the pillory, the galleys and more.

But he was to escape the whip and the nailing up by his ears to the pillory 'because he had betrayed his fellows'. Atkinson, however, was only one player in a grim drama that led to lives of misery in the Hull blockhouses for many others.

Most of these experts in sadism and torture were appointed by the notorious priest hater the Earl of Huntingdon, who held the title President of the North. Huntingdon held supreme authority and proved himself a cruel oppressor, described by one priest as little more than a monster.

A letter written in 1586 said of Huntingdon, who based himself at York: 'He is degenerated from all true nobility of his ancestors into a most bloody and heretical tyrant, insatiably thirsting for the lives and destruction of all good men, a fit instrument for the devil to work his will by...'

Huntingdon ruled – and in the Hull blockhouses and castle conditions grew worse for the imprisoned priests. One was to write: '...The tyrant's brutish malice hath neither end nor measure in afflicting those whom he hath caught within his reach.' The jailers were hand-picked by Huntingdon, many of them his own men who were 'promoted' to Hull after long service.

In Hull the conditions were awful. Catholic prisoners even had their water poisoned, and they were charged exorbitant amounts of money for their food, a point taken up by Father Edward Rishton, writing in 1580. He said:

'The Catholics incarcerated in the port or castle at Hull are detained in close custody, not allowed on any pretext to be visited, nor any help administered to them.' And another priest, writing in 1582, was to say that he knew of 14 'good men' who had been starved to death in Hull and York.

A document kept in archives in Rome gives a graphic account of life in the Hull blockhouses, referring to the 'many and great' punishments meted out there. Some men were kept three or four years in low houses without fire, their grim cells filling with water at high tide 'so that as they walked the earth was so raw and moist that their shoes would cleave to the ground'.

They were not allowed to speak to each other until their keepers allowed them to. 'The old Fathers, some of them falling sick and standing in great need of good looking to and help, were denied, and so pitifully died. Some of them had pegs in their legs and other infirmities through sickness, so that the chambers were corrupt and noisome...'

One man was said to have been 'monstrously abused' and condemned to have his ears cut off, a sentence which was carried out. 'Then the tyrants put him in a filthy place and prison called The Hall and kept him straitly, for he was thought to be a Catholic, and therefore they fined him, for he was glad to eat the crusts that some threw in at the window. Thus starving him he died and lay dead so long (how long none knoweth) that the rats had eaten his face and other places.'

Another priest held in the Hull blockhouses 'remained a close prisoner for three years in so moist a house that the grass did grow green in some parts'.

For others came total degradation, with one historian – Joseph H. Hirst – writing in his 1913 book *The Blockhouses of Hull and Who Went There*: 'The keeper was bidden by the Mayor to keep them without fire, light, beds or meat. In a moist low house in the North Blockhouse where there was no place of convenience John Fletcher and Michael Tyre were separated from all other company for the space of four years in the which time they had no other help for the needs of nature but to carry it forth in basins themselves into the water of the river... The said Michael did for the space of two or three years live

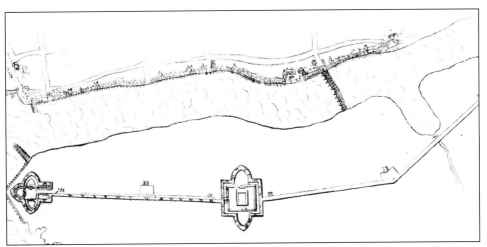

Where the blockhouses were situated. The southern blockhouse (left) is now the site of Hull's £45-million tourist attraction, The Deep.

without buying any other food excepting bread, penny ale and milk. He had already been a prisoner 20 years in 1594 and had not one day's liberty all that time.'

Many men died in the Hull blockhouses, some of them being buried in the churchyard at Drypool or under the castle walls. Women, too were imprisoned in Hull, like the men innocent of any crime. Their punishment was for their beliefs and for nothing else.

Riding high

Over the decades the East Riding has had its share of a different kind of hero – the horses and great horsemen who carved for themselves a place in history. Here we take a look at some of the animals, riders and owners that have put the county in the racing world's hall of fame.

It is the most famous race in Britain, if not the world. For over a century the Grand National has been a major sporting event, enjoyed by millions, a gruelling test of stamina and skill.

But it was an East Riding horse called Lottery who took the honours at the first ever Aintree event. He was a rather unlikely winner in the eyes of some, being dismissed as 'mealy brown, narrow and short in his quarters and not much to look at' when southern horse dealer John Elmore bought him at Horncastle Fair in Lincolnshire in 1836.

Seven years earlier Lottery had been bred by Mr Peter Jackson at White Cross near Leven and in 1834, under the name of Chance, he had won the Holderness Stakes, a flat race at the Holderness Hunt meeting. Elmore then sold him for riding with the staghounds in Norfolk and then brought him back for a trial over a steeplechase course. According to one spectator at the trial, 'That horse could jump from Hull to Hackney'. It was a wise prediction.

In 1839 Lottery began his great association with the jockey Jem Mason and in that same year, at his first attempt, he won the National. The following year he fell, in 1841 and 1842 he finished unplaced and in 1843 he ran again, without success. But that first race had made him a legend.

Lottery the wonder horse developed a 'leg' and ended his days peaceably doing light work on a farm. An East Riding village pub carries in its name a lasting memory of a horse which has a place in racing history.

The Altisodora pub at Bishop Burton remembers a horse which in 1813 went to Doncaster to win for his owner Richard Watt of that same village the legendary St Leger. That success was one of four which went to horses from Watt's stable. Barefoot took the St Leger honours in 1823, Memmon repeated it two years later and Rockingham romped home on the Doncaster course in 1833.

The Sykes family, of Sledmere, hold a long and lasting place in East Riding history. But through all the years one of the most amazing stories from a remarkable family must be that of Sir Tatton Sykes's journey to the St Leger at Doncaster in 1817.

From Sledmere he journeyed to Aberdeen, with his racing jacket under his waistcoat and a clean shirt and razor in his pocket, for the sake of a mount on the Marquis of Huntly's horse Kutusoff, when the Welter Stakes was the greatest race in Scotland. Without stopping even to dine the determined Yorkshireman went back to sleep at Breeching for the night and then set out for Doncaster – a six-day ride. He arrived at the course just in time to see his horse Blacklock beaten at the post.

The 360-mile journey was done mainly in the mornings on a little brood mare which one writer of the time said 'with the exception of a slight stiffness seemed no worse...'

The remarkable Sir Tatton once rode 63 miles in one morning to take second place in the Macaroni Stakes at Pontefract in the afternoon, slept at Doncaster that night and was only just beaten in a four-mile race at Lincoln the next day by a man known as 'Split-Post Douglas'.

Another old East Riding family with a great fascination for horses were the Constables of Holderness. Under the leadership of Sir Clifford Constable the Holderness Hunt races, which once were held at Beverley, were revived in the 1840s over a course laid out in the grounds of the historic Burton Constable Hall.

It was recorded at the time that 'Sir Clifford and Lady Constable, to add greater éclat to the end of the hunting season, continue to open their fine old mansion to their numerous friends when all the hospitalities for which Burton Constable is famous have ample outdoor sports to occupy the mornings of the visitors, and in the evenings music and private theatricals prove a source of much pleasure and amusement.'

What was not of such pleasure and amusement was an incident in 1838 when three pairs of Holderness hounds ran over Speeton Cliffs after they had run a fox from near

Burton Agnes. Three plunged over 200ft and were killed instantly, but hunt followers peering cautiously over the cliff edge could see that the other three were still alive, having landed on a ledge not so far below.

Huntmaster Tom Hodgson looked on in horror as his beloved hounds headed for the sheer drop, and unable to bear to watch turned his horse and set off for home. But Ned Oxtoby, the first whipper-in, was not so minded and volunteered to be lowered over the cliff. It was a dangerous moment, but he managed to bring two of the dogs to safety. The third, named Romulus, could not be reached.

The hunt set off for home and while on the journey huntsman Will Webb noticed the pack greeting a new arrival. It was Romulus, who had somehow managed to make his own way up from the ledge and who lived to hunt for many another day.

Hero of the Humber

It was quite a gathering. There were local worthies aplenty and well-to-do residents of Hull in their droves. And ordinary folk, too, all of them packed into the Music Hall in Jarratt Street.

They met that day to pay tribute to a man who became a legend for his life-saving prowess. More than any other he truly deserved the title Hero of the Humber...

For centuries the ferries that plied the Humber helped bring trade and prosperity to Hull. They were an historic institution, it having been in 1316 that Edward II agreed to a request from the burgesses of Hull to establish a ferry across the river from Barton. Its purpose, according to historian James Sheahan, was 'to bring and carry over men, horses, beasts etc at the rate of one halfpenny for every single person, a penny for every horseman and two pence for every cart going across with two horses'.

The grant was made to the wardens and burgesses, their heirs and successors 'for ever'. Five hundred years after that proclamation the ferry was a regular and important part of the commercial life of the Humber. By then it was run by a Mr Ellerthorpe, who had come to the area from Rawcliffe. It was a job he loved and for 40 years he plied the Humber as ferryman. It was not, however, an easy way of making a living, for the Humber is a dangerous estuary with hidden hazards even for those who fully appreciate the complexities of navigating its swirling waters, cross currents and sandbanks.

Ellerthorpe was well aware of the dangers of the river and knew its mood swings well.

But even he could not have foreseen the night when a sudden gale sprang up, whipping up the waves which began to rock the ferry violently as it made its crossing.

Suddenly the boat lurched, the old man lost his grip and was thrown into the cold, swirling and muddy water. With Ellerthorpe on the boat that night in 1820 was his 14-year-old son, John, who, on realising what had happened, acted instinctively, leaping into the angry waters. When he saw his father rise to the surface he seized hold of him and, despite his youth, managed with great difficulty to drag him back to the boat.

The boy was unable to haul his father aboard, but was strong enough to swim to the shore, where he summoned help. It was a dramatic and heroic rescue and for John Ellerthorpe it was the first incident in an amazing career in which he saved the lives of 39 people. Sheahan would write of him: 'Each of the persons that Ellerthorpe has saved from a watery grave was rescued by himself single handedly by instantly plunging into the water and this has not been effected without great danger. No, this extraordinary man has had several hair breadth escapes...'

During his career John Ellerthorpe saved the lives of three little girls, five youths, six women and 15 men on the night of 19 November 1835 when he was working as watchman on board the New Holland packet.

Conditions on the river were dreadful as gales raged across the region, bringing with them blinding showers of sleet. The ferry had moored and Ellerthorpe was making her safe for the night when he heard a splash. It was made by a man who had fallen into the water. Ellerthorpe, with little regard for his own safety, dived straight in, managing to pull the man to the steps at the end of the pier, an act which was later said to have taken so much out of him that he could well have died of exhaustion had not the ship's engineer helped him home.

In Hull news of the rescue spread like wildfire, the result being that Ellerthorpe was offered – and accepted – a fee of two pounds a week to walk around the pier and docks and be ready to rescue anyone who fell into the water. But it was not just in the Humber that Ellerthorpe achieved fame for his courage and determination as a lifesaver. There were other rescues that attracted widespread attention.

On one occasion he jumped overboard after a shipmate – he sailed as a seaman on coasters trading between Hull and London for a time – who had fallen into the Thames from the bow of a brig. An account of the rescue said: 'He seized the drowning man and was carried with him under two tier of ships by the strong ebb tide running down the river.'

And in Quebec Ellerthorpe carried out one of his most amazing rescues of all. A man who had fallen into the harbour had around his neck the chains which were used to fasten timber into the raft on which he had been working. 'But in spite of the man's heavy load Ellerthorpe succeeded in bringing him from under the raft,' said one account. In the same harbour he brought up, from a depth of 25ft, a brother seaman who had leaped overboard in a state of intoxication. And on another occasion he was taken out of the paddle wheel of a steamboat unconscious.

Throughout his life Ellerthorpe was adamant that he would not accept a reward from those he had rescued. But there was to be one exception. A woman who had fallen off the bridge and into the water at the dock gate had been rescued by Ellerthorpe. As was his custom he refused her offer of a gift.

But according to one record: 'The following Christmas she astonished Ellerthorpe by calling at his house and presenting him with a duck. He knew that she was too poor to afford such a luxury and therefore he refused to accept the present, saying her gratitude was sufficient reward for what he had done.

'She, however, was not of his way of thinking and declared that she had intended all along to buy him a goose, but not having sufficient money had been forced to content herself with a duck. Under the circumstances it was impossible to refuse and for the only time in his life Ellerthorpe accepted a reward from the person he had rescued.'

He did, however, accept awards presented to him as tribute to his courage.

After saving a boy sailor from drowning in 1835 the Royal Humane Society awarded him their silver medal and a certificate on vellum and the people of Hull took the opportunity to mark their admiration of him.

Subscriptions totalling £197 10s, which included £20 donated by the Prime Minister, Lord Palmerston, out of the Royal Bounty, were raised and Ellerthorpe was presented with a purse containing 100 guineas and a gold watch and guard.

John Ellerthorpe died in 1868 at the age of 62. His funeral was attended by hundreds of people, many of whom travelled to Hull from different parts of the country to pay their respects to a remarkable man.

Hero, villain
— or both?

No one would deny that James Acland was a troublemaker. It was his stock in trade and it brought to the streets of Hull discontent which flared into riot.

Later described as a 'mob leader,' Acland was a 19th-century firebrand, a rebel with – he believed – a cause worth fighting for. That was to oppose authority. One historian would write: 'He attacked every institution, and every individual member of each institution, but to make war against the corporation of the town seemed to be his chief aim... He succeeded in bringing the citizens of this hitherto quiet old town to the verge of rebellion...'

Acland descended on an unsuspecting town in the summer of 1831 and soon established himself as the self-styled champion of popular liberty. He was a rebel, a villain and, to many, a hero...

The authorities were worried. Very worried indeed. On the streets there was talk of rebellion. The people were angry and the threat of violence hung heavy in the air. Months of agitation had brought to the fore years of dissatisfaction.

Desperate to find a way out of a situation they feared could destroy the social structure of the town, officials met to discuss what action they could take. The result: 800 special constables were sworn in to help keep the peace. And all because of the activities of James Acland.

Acland arrived in Hull after working as an actor, a teacher in France and a lecturer on

This was Myton Bridge in Hull in Acland's time – around 1830. The picture first appeared as a wood cut in his publication, Hull Portfolio.

Shakespeare and phrenology. He was quick-witted, cunning and eloquent, soon gaining the attention of townspeople with his forthright views and determined stand against anyone in authority for whatever reason he chose.

'Those who believed in his honesty and patriotism looked upon him as a thorough radical reformer, devoting all his energies with an extraordinary zeal towards redressing what he conceived to be the wrongs of the people. Others believed him to be simply an interested agitator,' said one writer.

It took only a few weeks for Acland, a superb self-publicist, to first stir unrest. The date was 1 November 1831. Following his arrival in the town it had not taken Acland long to question the legality of market tolls charged by the Corporation. There was only one way to mount a challenge, he decided, and that was by direct action.

So he set to work, persuading stall keepers to refuse to pay the tolls and going into business himself to show he was prepared to lead from the front. Acland set up a stall of his own in front of the King William statue. For sale were eggs, cards and his own publication, the *Hull Portfolio,* which was similar in its content to an earlier paper he had produced in Bristol, where he lived before moving to Hull. That had landed him in trouble with the law and eventually earned him a prison term for libel.

The stall proved popular, receiving wide support from the public, and it was recorded that 'the crowding and excitement witnessed on that occasion in the Market Place is well remembered...'

Further fuel was added to the campaign by another ruse – selling gingerbread figures of the mayor, J.B. Briggs, and aldermen of the town. But this was small-time agitation. Acland had bigger ideas and started to put them into practice.

He turned now to the Humber ferry service. Acland looked with interest at this essential link between the banks of the estuary and decided that the monopoly of the service owners should – in the best interests of the public, of course, be broken.

The best way of doing this, he decided, was for a rival service to be created and that was what he did. Acland bought a boat called the *Aire*, renamed it *Public Opinion*, and went into business, his vessel flying a unique flag which carried the corporation arms upside down.

The service was an undoubted success. Acland's steamboat plied between Barton and Hull and he charged his passengers a much lower rate than his rival. The fare to Barton and back was one shilling, and his advice was that it was not worth more than a halfpenny. The Acland 'revolution' was rolling. And there was much more to come. Next in line were the tolls paid to cross Hull's bridges, which linked the east and west sides of the town. Acland toured them all, refusing to pay the tolls and then creating an anti-toll association. It was that which led to such serious concern among those responsible for law and order that hundreds of special constables were recruited.

By now the Corporation had suffered enough. Meetings in the Town Hall decided on a course of action – and Acland found himself once again the subject of a libel writ. But the hearing, in the King's Bench, which was due to take place in February 1832, was adjourned. Acland returned to Hull in triumph.

So strong was public support for him that an estimated 20,000 people turned out to welcome him back. Music played and banners were raised as he paraded through the town heading for the Market Place, where, from a balcony, he harangued the crowd.

But there was more involvement with the law to follow. On the last day of March that year a court in York heard the case concerning the Barton ferry and Acland's attempts to smash the monopoly. He was found guilty, but escaped lightly, being ordered to pay damages of only one farthing. But there was a problem. Costs for the case amounted to £270 and Acland could not afford that sort of money.

So he did what he knew best – and took action for himself, barricading himself in his house in Queen Street in a vain attempt to avoid arrest.

May 1832

In the Town Hall serious-faced men gathered to share their thoughts on just what could be done about the problems posed by James Acland. He was a rabble rouser, a dangerous agitator who simply had to be contained, continually demanding changes not only to local regulations, but also agitating for parliamentary reform. Heads shook with disgust as they reflected on his efforts. This was, they heard, the man who in 1831 at a meeting called by 'local gentlemen of great respectability' had assembled a rabble of the 'lower classes' and then delivered a long and antagonistic speech about the aristocracy. Such people were, according to Acland, 'the locusts of the state'. As for bishops, for whom he also had little regard, they were dismissed as 'the agents of the anti-Christ'. This, plus his various attempts to take on the authorities and discredit those who ran the town, was simply too much. Action was needed – and fast.

The Corporation, determined to end the Acland problem once and for all, filed another declaration against him in what it hoped would resolve the issue over tolls. But Acland was not a man to take such things lightly and fought back, organising a fighting fund for himself and managing to cajole £250 out of stallholders. It was a brave, if ill-founded effort, for he finally finished up in jail for not paying the costs of the ferry trial the previous February.

More trouble followed. Acland was next convicted for libelling one of the trustees of a local charity. And in this he was able to demonstrate his ability as an advocate, being said to have defended himself 'with considerable ingenuity and had several altercations with the judges in which he displayed a great knowledge of the law and an amount of tact not often possessed by unprofessional men'.

But these setbacks did not deter a man like Acland. He fought back, his next move being to offer himself for office as Chamberlain of the Corporation, the election for which led to noisy scenes and forced the mayor to order that Acland be taken into custody and the military be called out to keep the peace.

He also fancied his chances as a Member of Parliament, offering himself as a candidate in a general election in the new parliamentary borough of Kingston-upon-Hull, created by the Reform Act of 1832. Historian James Sheahan takes up the story:

'The peaceable and well disposed portion of the townspeople then suffered great annoyance from the disorderly assemblies drawn together by his nightly harangues and frequent processions. Above 500 gentlemen signed a declaration that "viewing with alarm the state of riot and disorder at present prevailing" by which "their lives and property were endangered and the peace of the town placed in imminent jeopardy" they were determined by every means in their power "to support the magistracy in all legal and proper measures which they may think it right to adopt for repressing these violent and disorderly hearings".'

For Acland such things were of little importance. Undeterred, he then opened a small shop at No.23 Queen Street. And to demonstrate that there was no change whatever in his views on how Hull was run he called it 'The Anti-Corporative Castle'. Here he sold a variety of items which reflected that name – among them 'Public Opinion Coffee', 'Anti-Corporate Tea' and 'Radical Tobacco'. But his popularity was waning and the days when Acland was a powerful force were beginning to run out, although he did still command a large following, enough for it to be said that 'although his popularity was on the wane riots and disorder prevailed in the town to a very great extent'.

November 1832 saw Acland back in jail, this time in Bury St Edmunds, where he faced an 18-month sentence for libel. But, it would be recorded, 'his vituperation still went forth from the prison through the pages of the *Portfolio* and though incarcerated he still persisted in becoming a candidate at the next election for MPs to represent Hull'.

The election took place in December 1832 and although unable to actively campaign Acland managed to win 433 votes. But his hour of glory was now over and although he made several appeals from prison for help his old friends and admirers turned their backs on him.

Sheahan would write: 'The first of October 1834 would find him writing from the Hull gaol asking his followers, if any were left for assistance in his hour of need but his day had passed, his best friends had become his enemies; the mask had fallen; the charm was broken and Acland's occupation was gone...'

Schoolroom villains preyed on the young

The history of any town is littered with the actions of the unscrupulous wreaking havoc on the lives of the unwary. Hull is no exception.

The 19th century saw the horrific activities of both landlords and so-called teachers who between them did nothing to help the unfortunates with whom they had contact. Both were, in their own way, villains of a particularly nasty kind, preying on the poor, the sick, the young and the old...

Not much is known about Mr D.J. O'Donoghue. He was without doubt, though, a conscientious worker as clerk to the Hull School Board, thorough, hard working and a man of deep social conscience.

It was in November and December 1879 that Mr O'Donoghue came into his own as an official to be taken notice of and respected. For that was when in his own words he was 'busily engaged in visiting any and every building that could possibly be called a school'.

And, as he was paid by results, he was fully aware of the need to ensure that none was missed. During his investigation into conditions at these so-called teaching establishments the resolute Mr O'Donoghue visited over 200 elementary schools in the town and also about 50 others 'whose proprietors stated they charged more than ninepence a week'.

What he found was appalling. The young were the victims of greedy villains who took every penny they could, often from parents who could not afford it, and provided nothing in return.

Conditions in many of the schools, known as 'dame schools', were dreadful. Usually over-crowded, there was an 'almost total lack of sanitary arrangements and the whole of the so-called instruction, except in a comparatively few cases, was simply deplorable'. The investigation revealed a cynical disregard for education by people who knowingly and willingly exploited their young charges.

A school in the Commercial Road area was typical. It was kept by a poor widow in her own living room. 'She had lost the roof of her mouth, consequently it was difficult for a time to understand what she said. She had five or six scholars, from each of whom she received two pence per week, but for boys of nine or 10 years of age she charged three pence. She said she taught reading and scripture and writing on slates at times, but there was neither a reading book nor slate in the place.'

The young victims of such people did not stand a chance.

Proceedings were taken against the parents of one young victim of a so-called school. Their daughter, aged 11, simply knew nothing at all. Her parents found themselves charged with not sending their child to an efficient school.

The widow who ran this alleged educational establishment was a crook who really did prey on the innocent. She admitted to signing the return for her school with a cross 'because her writing was not very good'. And the magistrate who heard the case found he could scarcely make out some of her statements on account of a defect on the roof of her mouth.

The magistrate, it seemed, was about as good at administering the law as the 'teacher' was at helping children. He came to the strange conclusion that the girl was receiving 'efficient instruction in some other manner' at the establishment. The reason for this perverse logic – the girl was totally ignorant, and although her teacher did not know very much she knew considerably more than her pupil. The case was dismissed, in Mr O'Donoghue's view, purely out of sympathy with the poor widow.

At a school near Hull Town Hall the old lady who ran the place was simply known as 'mam'. Mr O'Donoghue would report: 'The room was so dreadfully small that when the forms were set to receive the children, they occupied nearly the full length of the room, so much so, that the door which fronted the street could only be partially opened and the children at the end of the forms were close upon the fire. Beside this there were one or two chairs, a little round table and not much else except a fine cane and a well used churchwarden pipe.

'The old lady was smoking when I arrived and as she was so dreadfully deaf it was with the greatest difficulty I could obtain information from her. I learned that she was in receipt of parish relief. She could neither read nor write, nor did she profess to teach anybody to do so, although she had in her window a very ancient looking bill, splendidly spotted with fly specks containing the following – 'Mrs —-'s day school'.

He asked her to sign a form and she did so with a large cross, breaking the pen in the attempt. Such was the state of 'schools' in Hull.

There were in fact 50 or 60 such establishments at one time, a great many of them run by crooks or illiterates. Their victims were the innocents they allegedly taught.

Victim of trench 'justice'

In the hell of the trenches of World War One no one was hated more than the deserters, the soldiers who refused to fight or to go 'over the top'. They were reviled, despised, tried – and shot.

This true story of a Yorkshireman who could not face the enemy across the muddy wastes of No Man's Land reflects one such case of front line 'justice'.

Some may have branded him a coward. Others saw him as he really was – a victim of mental illness who could not fully comprehend his situation. And who died at the hands of his colleagues in khaki as a result.

For Len Cavinder, like the tens of hundreds of others who flocked to Hull City Hall to enlist, the reality was a far cry from what had been promised. It was October 1915. He signed for duty with the 4th East Yorkshire Regiment. And went to France.

Sixty-seven years later Len Cavinder told about his war in a tape recorded interview. And in particular he told of one incident which is today a sad and grim reflection on British military justice. It was recorded in the magazine *Gun Fire*, produced by members of the Western Front Association in York in the mid-1980s.

'When we were at Arras Front I was dishing out the rations for the day. It was two boiled rabbits between three men. It was July 1917. I got to the end of the trench and there were only two men left so they were able to have a cold rabbit each. Nobody had been killed during the night. There had been nobody wounded and I had to report the last man... so

I reported it. He wasn't found until six months later in St Omer a long way back. He'd deserted. Major Jackson, of Hull, he came along to me and said "I want you to look after so and so who is going to be shot for desertion. I want you to fetch him from Brandhoek, near Ypres to Ypres gaol". Ten men of my platoon who were in the front line had to come out to Ypres gaol every day for target practice. They had to fire at a small piece of paper. Five knelt down, five stood up. They were laced with an extra ration of rum. They knew what (it was all about) but they were sworn to silence. Nobody had to know.'

Recalling the prisoner he and a colleague, a man called Danby, went to collect Mr Cavinder said: 'He was subnormal actually. He was unstable. There was something wrong with him. I realised that you couldn't get him to slope his arms correctly. He wasn't simple, but he was slow, but he'd not been slow enough to live with this woman in St Omer for six months. In the gaol I was given half a bottle of whisky and two laudanum tablets. I was to give these to him. I wish he had all the whisky but he was aware that something was afoot but we were not to tell him.'

Midnight. And the heavy tramp of boots echoed through the dim and dingy building. One by one they entered, red tabbed officers, grim-faced men with a terrible message to impart. They stopped and one held up a single sheet of paper, reading its message slowly and deliberately... The deserter was to die, to be shot at dawn.

There was no ceremony, no visible sign on any of their faces that suggested what was about to happen may have been ranked as injustice, nor was there any suggestion that the soldier might appeal. 'They trooped out. He was like a raving maniac for a while and then he settled down... he got his photographs out and started to hum a song. Then in came the padre whom we only very occasionally saw', said Mr Cavinder.

From this man of God came not words of kindness nor of comfort. At the doorway Len Cavinder looked on in disbelief as the padre spoke. 'I heard every word he said. He was telling the chap that he deserved to die and that he would go to Hell if he didn't ask for God's forgiveness. I saw red and I went barging in and I said "Excuse me sir but I've been asked to help this fellow to find God, but I don't think that's the way to do it." He said "All right, sergeant, I'll report you." That's the last time I ever saw that parson.'

Instead it was Cavinder who stayed with the man, comforting him, praying with him, encouraging him to kneel as together they prayed. 'He was almost raving at times because he knew what was coming. Then he calmed down. I don't know whether it was the effects of the whisky, but I don't think he'd had enough to affect him.'

For hour after long and lonely hour the vigil continued. 'It was seven o'clock. It was just becoming daylight when in came two military police. They put a respirator on him – the bag kind, and turned the eye pieces round and the mouth piece so that he could see nothing. They pinned a piece of paper, the size which those fellows had shot at when they were making a target... they pinned that on his chest and manacled his arms behind him and before they fastened the manacles I shook hands with him and said "God bless you..."

'They just took him round the corner of the cell to the wall and there were my 10 platoon men. I knew every one of them personally. Five knelt down, five stood up and as soon as he was... oh, no, they strapped him on a chair with his hands still behind the back of the chair. And there he sat until one of our officers gave the order "Fire" and that was it.'

Cavinder recalled that stretcher bearers ordered to put the man in his grave would not do the job so it was left to him and Danby. 'We lifted him into the hole, dropped him in the hole. It was December and the yard was frost hard, icy. I could only get clumps of clay and we dropped, both of us, started to drop earth on him... It was a sorry affair and those 10 men, none of them knew who shot him because five were given blank cartridges and five were live and they were given the rifles as they took their place so they had no feelings of guilt. And that was that.'

Heroes, villains
— and victims

On the fishing grounds drink was the answer to most men's problems. Or so fishermen liked to believe. The Dutch and Germans were quick to exploit the situation, selling or bartering vast amounts of liquor to the English fishing fleet.

Frequently crews were drunk to a man, with even the skipper being unable to take control of his vessel. It was a problem which eventually began to concern the late 19th-century smack owners, but not before it had taken a dreadful toll of men and vessels.

There were cases of men falling overboard and drowning as a result of drinking bouts. Sometimes because the entire crew was drunk a boy apprentice with little or no seagoing experience would have to take command of the boat.

But even without drink conditions on the smacks were dreadful. Injured men died or suffered in agony when wounded while working until land was reached. Brutality was commonplace and in the sailing days few dared to complain. Even those who did were not listened to.

One writer recorded: 'Foul deeds could be so easily concealed. Many dreadful crimes were committed for which no punishment could be inflicted, because the perpetrators were not known. But occasionally there would come to light some wrong of exceptional character which would be dealt with by a judge and jury and give the public an insight into the lives of deep sea toilers who were more outcasts from their fellow creatures ashore than the heathen in far countries.'

These cases tell of heroes, villains and victims of the early fishing fleet, men and boys who courted death as part of their everyday working lives.

The wound was severe. Blood ran freely as the boy screamed in pain, his arm torn open from elbow to wrist. Fellow crewmen rushed to see what had happened, wrapping cloth around the wound in a desperate attempt to staunch the flow of blood. Miraculously they succeeded, but the wound, raw and open, was agonising.

For 16 weeks a young boy lived in agony, unable to receive proper medical help. And even when they finally returned to port he had to go back to the fleet almost immediately and leave the healing process to nature and to chance. He survived, as did others who were also subjected to treatment of the roughest and most primitive kind.

It was a time when human life was cheap, when drunken brutality ruled. In the early days of the industry it was believed that a mixture of treacle and turpentine was a suitable and efficient medicine for most injuries, when, as one writer would say, 'fine lads and splendid men who had been cruelly wounded in their calling had to endure inexpressible torture in a rolling, wallowing storm-hammered smack or carrier before harbour could be reached – and then the flag at half mast would tell the sorry tale too late'.

Drink drove many fishermen to commit crimes.

The curse of the North Sea fleets were the copers or coopers, vessels which for over 50 years sailed from Continental ports to sell drink and tobacco to English fishermen. Out of this developed a bartering system – one which brought ruin to many skippers and their crews.

One writer said: 'The evil of bartering grew so much that in the worst days of the coper an established system of wrong doing existed and it sometimes happened that the skipper, in order to satisfy his craving for drink, would dispose of all his gear and even, in extreme cases, the smack itself.'

On the sailing boat *Annie* there was a mood of wellbeing. The crew were relaxed and happy carrying out their duties in a carefree way as the vessel drove steadily towards the coast, by now clearly visible in the bright air of early morning.

Pushed along by a strengthening wind the craft made good and steady progress, eventually arriving in port in the early afternoon. Within hours she was fully laden, her cargo of cigarettes, tobacco and drink carefully stowed below decks.

To those who had seen the *Annie* leaving the Humber there was no clue as to the real

Emptying a net of fish on board a Hull fishing trawler.

purpose of her voyage. Indeed, they could well have been forgiven for assuming that, like a hundred similar craft which used the river that particular day, she had no other intention than to travel to or from the rich North Sea fishing grounds which had become known as the Silver Pit.

For the skipper who had bought his boat only a few months previously, fishing was no life, and certainly not one that would make him a rich man. There were, he had rapidly realised, richer pickings elsewhere. In the Dutch port of Nieudiep the *Annie* was quickly laden with her precious cargo, the skipper watching carefully as tobacco and grog worth over £500 was taken aboard.

Within a few hours she was ready for the sea again, departing quietly and soon establishing an anchorage on the Dogger Bank where she lay still, watching and waiting as the ever-growing collection of similar vessels worked all around her.

Gutting the fish aboard a trawler.

Her unannounced arrival was soon noticed and it was not long before small boats were lowered from neighbouring smacks to make their way towards her. The *Annie* was in business, a lucrative one which would double her skipper's investment in a two-month trip, bringing far richer rewards than he could ever expect from a fishing voyage.

Trade, as always, was good and there was no question in the skipper's mind that what he was doing would lead in some cases to violence and even death.

A bottle of rum would sell for 1s 6d, raw brandy brought 2s, aniseed brandy – a dangerous and insidious spirit which could create in men mood swings from lethargy to extreme violence – for just 2s 3d, and gin – ever the favourite with many – just one shilling.

It was a trade in which there were no rules and certainly no morals. But it would bring him a profit of around 600 percent a year, infinitely more than could be made out of the most successful trawling.

But the system of copering, so far as English vessels were concerned, was never to become fully established or permanent. The authorities, normally slow to react, were only too aware of the dangers that drink could create on the fishing grounds and pressure was brought to bear, particularly from insurance clubs in England, who made it clear that smacks which sailed under the guise of fishing boats to hawk drink and tobacco were not wanted.

The *Annie's* days as a trader in anything other than fish, like others tempted by the lure of fast profits at the cost of men's dignity and lives, were soon over.

Fate of the
fisher-lads

'Next witness.'

The Rt Hon Joseph Chamberlain nodded to the usher who turned and left the packed, warm room, glad to be given the opportunity to take in some fresh air as he walked into the corridor to summon a short, stocky man, beckoning him towards the door. The man entered, looked around at a sea of faces and walked slowly towards the stand.

Chamberlain, chairman of the inquiry, the evidence from which would help shape the policies of his forthcoming Merchant Shipping Bill, called for silence.

'What is your name,' he inquired of the witness.

'Henry Toozes of Hull,' came the reply.

'I did not catch that,' declared the statesman. 'Hull? Did you say Hull?'

'Yes,' replied Toozes, an alderman of that town, a well-known and respected figure.

'Oh yes, we all know Hull,' said Chamberlain.

'That's where they murder fisher boys...'

They were children without hope, bashed, beaten, used and abused. Many tried to run away from cruel and callous masters who regarded them more as animals than teenagers struggling to eke out an existence.

They were the fisher boys of Hull and Grimsby, youngsters without homes or in many cases families, thrown into a burgeoning industry where life came cheap and brutality was rife.

Ashore in Hull after trips on North Sea fishing smacks these young apprentices were often left to fend for themselves until their boats sailed again. They were the vulnerable and often innocent victims of a system which saw ruthless masters and waterfront thugs force boys into lives of misery. In the dockland areas prostitution, drinking and violence were commonplace. Brothels abounded and a youngster who had made a pitiful living while at sea soon found himself parted from his money.

It was a situation which caused mounting concern in official quarters, and one which tempted the journalist Richard Cooke, editor and owner of the *Hull Critic*, to investigate the facts of life in Hull's less than salubrious areas.

In a series entitled 'Hull After Dark' he visited many of the hovels that abounded in the early 1890s, among them those in Bowlalley Lane in the heart of the Old Town, now at the centre of the legal and professional area of the city. This is what he found:

We enter one of the houses and first see a dirty old man with limbs as crooked as his heart and mind. For many years he has got a living from the prostitution of women and the illicit sale of drink and is well known to the police as having more girls on his premises than any other den in the locality.

The licensing laws do not affect his property and the "time gentlemen" of the respectable vendor of alcohol is there an unknown tongue. There are several females in the room, some young and some middle aged, but all with dissipation and vice plainly indicated in their soddened features. They are the lowest of the low, against whom some of the unfortunates of the town appear as angels of light.

The language of one young woman is most horrible. She is called by her companions Saucy Poll on account of her vile tongue. Every sentence she uses is a disgrace to her sex and you leave the house ashamed of the fact that you are her fellow creature.

We now cross to the other side of the passage and in a house there find a procuress, her bully and a girl about 17 or 18 years of age waiting for a 'mark'.

As young as the girl is she has already got the stamp of her character on her face, while it is difficult to say which is the most filthy, her tongue or her hands.

...Not only are prostitution and drunkenness rampant in this neighbourhood, but robbery is rife. Dozens of poor misguided sailors go there after a long voyage, are made intoxicated, filched of their undoubtedly extremely hard-earned

'Water's comin...' the warning shout would send smacksmen running for cover, usually down the ladder and below decks into a cabin like this one.

money, assaulted and turned out into the street without the slightest means of making provision for the next voyage...

Whether 15-year-old William Papper was a frequenter of such places is unknown. But as a typical fisher-lad of the early 1880s he was nevertheless a victim of a ruthless and cruel apprenticeship system – and one whose name lives on in one of the most infamous cases ever to involve members of the Hull fishing community. William and five shipmates sailed from Hull on 16 December 1881 aboard the fishing smack *Rising Sun*. He never returned.

The trouble began before the vessel sailed: a chance remark, made innocently, which led to murder. William was talking to his skipper, Osmond Otto Brand and his wife. During their conversation the boy told Brand: 'My sister Emma knows you'. Whether this implied more than a bare suggestion of knowledge or a greater degree of intimacy is unknown. Mrs Brand said nothing but the skipper seethed. It was shortly after the *Rising Sun* sailed, jutting down the Humber towards the North Sea fishing grounds, that he first raised the matter, telling William: 'I will pay you out for telling lies', before describing what had happened to a member of his crew. It was not long before Brand put his threat into action.

The dark interior of a typical cabin on an old fishing smack. Besides the table with folding sides there were lockers, with bunks above them.

The morning after sailing, when anchored off Sunk Island, Brand sent William below and, following him, declared: 'I have done for your sister; now I will do for you.' Lashing out with a knotted rope an inch and a half thick he thrashed the boy unmercifully, smashing him repeatedly over the head and face, swearing loudly as the blows fell. It was the beginning of a terrible end for William Papper. Blows inflicting serious injuries increased on the boy, day after terrible day. Food was denied him. Time and again he fell into unconsciousness.

For a time William stood up to his ordeal but finally he succumbed and lapsed into unconsciousness. Brand reacted by forcing hot tea and tobacco into his mouth in an attempt to bring him round, but to no avail. Brand acted swiftly, having the boy's body thrown into the sea, then telling the other apprentice that William had fallen overboard. And that, believed the skipper, was that.

On returning to Hull he never reported the death to the police, who were only made aware of William's murder some time later when a member of the *Rising Sun* crew, in a fit of conscience, told what had happened.

Brand was arrested and taken to the police station in Parliament Street, a scene witnessed by a *Hull Daily Mail* reporter who later recalled:

Smile please. With a broad grin a North Sea skipper poses for the camera wearing his 'dopper' or blanket overall.

> *Brand was brought in by Detective Superintendent Trafford. He was a smart little fellow and moreover was well liked by the Hull fishermen.*
>
> *If he had been guilty of half the acts which were alleged against him he was one of the most heartless of men but certainly his manner throughout his trial did not convey that impression.*
>
> *The case aroused considerable feeling in Hull and the witnesses even had to be lodged at the Central Police Station during the several weeks it lasted.*

At the end of the hearing Brand was sentenced to death by Mr Justice Williams and went to the gallows at Armley Gaol on 23 May 1882.

Torture at sea

In the midsummer heat the mood in the courtroom was sombre as the judge addressed the man standing before him. Calmly, his voice stern, he delivered the sentence – death by hanging. Justice had been seen to be done.

Coming just two months after Brand had been hanged for the murder of William Papper the case of Peter Hughes again highlighted the plight of boys who worked on Hull fishing vessels.

Peter was the victim of Edward Wheatfield, who was the second hand aboard the smack *Gleaner* and, it was said, was a man who did not respond to orders from the skipper Daniel George, who appeared to have little control over him. Certainly no one appeared to have been able to prevent him from carrying out a series of sadistic attacks on the boy.

Hauling the trawl – fishermen at work in the North Sea.

Systematic beatings were regular, Peter being hit with a rope end and viciously kicked. Then he was stripped naked, being forced to walk the deck carrying a bucket of water on his head.

Hungry, tired, in pain and cold he was repeatedly denied food and was said at one time to have been persistently kicked by Wheatfield for three quarters of an hour, by which time his hands were bare to the bone. Other crew members did nothing to help and actually joined in the torture, one of them daubing the boy with his own excrement. Peter died after being thrown overboard.

As with the case of William Papper, the real reasons why Peter died did not come to light immediately, with Wheatfield claiming that the boy had fallen into the sea while drawing water on board.

The homecoming

Brutality ruled on the fishing smack *Sterling*. And the victim of the attentions of crewmen Joseph Nicholine and Thomas Hardisty was young apprentice Joseph Rowbottom.

Joseph was 15 years old. A Southampton boy, he was one of many who found their way to Hull and were drawn into the fishing industry. Joseph found himself serving as cook aboard the *Sterling*. As on many smacks in the early 1880s life for a boy on the *Sterling* was harsh. Long hours of boredom led to bullying and violence by other members of the crew. For Joseph it led to death.

In May 1884 Nicholine and Hardisty faced trial. After a two-day hearing the jury returned a verdict of manslaughter, ruling that both should be kept in penal servitude for the rest of their natural lives.

In May 1904 a chance encounter on the street brought a *Hull Times* reporter face-to-face with a man he had last seen 20 years earlier. He would later recall: 'Then he was a smart and dapper little skipper but 29 years of age. Today although not quite 50 his age would be guessed at anything between 60 and 70. He expressed great relief at his liberation but was very downcast that he was not a free man in the strict sense of the term. "I have only been allowed out on licence and I think it is very hard having served 20 years", he said. He had returned to Hull to look for his wife, although he did not know if she was alive or dead...'

Nicholine had faced two hard decades in several prisons, for 19 of those years working as a moulder in iron foundries. And his fellow killer?

'I never met him after we were convicted but I have been told that he committed suicide and was found dead', he told the paper.

Death on the Dogger Bank

At the corner of Hull's Hessle Road and The Boulevard stands a statue commemorating a remarkable event in that city's history. The figure of a fisherman, his right arm raised into the sky, commemorates a night of infamy which almost led Britain to war. The date was 22 October 1904, the place, the Dogger Bank. The victims, men of the Hull fishing fleet...

Two visitors (second and fifth left, back row) join the crew to pose for this picture taken aboard a North Sea mission ship.

On the peaceful fishing grounds of the North Sea the boats of the Hull fishing fleet bobbed gently on a light swell. There were three days to go before full moon in late October and the weather that autumn night was typical of the time of year, hazy with Scotch mist at times. But the lights of the ships were clearly visible as they worked on the Dogger Bank 200 miles east by north of Spurn in 23 fathoms of water.

These were the vessels of the Gamecock fleet, around 30 steam trawlers, a dozen of them belonging to Leyman and Company.

The Dogger was second home to the fleet, which had fished there for the past 10 years. Near the working vessels lay two others, hospital steamers of the Mission to Deep Sea Fishermen, and three carriers. And so they fished on, quietly and efficiently, their crews well rehearsed in their work. It was a peaceful night, punctuated only by the sound of men calling out to each other, joking, easy in the company of shipmates who knew each other well. On some vessels men, exhausted after hours of hard work, tried to sleep, dreaming of well earned shore leave, of seeing their families, of the Hull pubs. And then the Russians arrived.

The Baltic Fleet was travelling in two sections down the North Sea having sailed from Libau on 15 October in pursuit of the Japanese Navy when, shortly before midnight on the 22nd, it came across the vessels of the Gamecock Fleet. One section of warships passed with no more than a cursory glance at the vessels, searchlights dancing across the cold, dark waters to highlight them.

The second – four battleships – steamed across the head of the trawlers and from one of the ships came the noise of a bugle. In seconds, gun crews reacted... and for 20 minutes the boats of the Gamecock Fleet became the centre of an international incident.

For several minutes the hail of shells, shot and rifle calibre bullets ripped the fishing fleet apart. And when the attack ended men on the trawlers lay dead and seriously injured. One vessel, the *Crane,* was sunk and five others, the *Mino, Moulmein, Gull, Snipe* and *Majestic* were damaged by shots. Others also received damage due to the explosion of shells close to them.

One of the men from the *Crane* would later tell the grim facts of a terrible night:

We were in the fish pound cleaning the fish and passing jokes about the war vessels which we could see quite plain and heard their firing when something hit us.

We were hit again and someone called out and said the bosun was shot. I went to look and found him bleeding and a hole through our bulwarks and the fore companionway knocked away.

I went to tell the skipper but before I got aft a shot went through the engine casing. I went past the chief who was bleeding, gave him my neckcloth to stop the blood and saw the skipper lying on the grating. I picked him up and saw his head was battered to pieces. I dropped him, rushed down the forecastle and saw the boatswain lying on the floor with his head battered in...

Then another shot hit them, men by now panicking in the mayhem. Nearby the *Gull* put a boat down which inched across the water, searchlights blazing down from the

A deck view of the hospital steamer Joseph and Sarah Miles, *which was on the scene to help the injured following the Dogger Bank incident.*

warships making the whole scene surreal and unbelievable.

The attack over and over 300 shells discharged, the Russians sped past. And on the fishing grounds the Hull fleet counted its dead and wounded. From the mission ship *Joseph and Sarah Miles*, commanded by Skipper White, the surgeon Dr Anklesaria went to the *Gull* to see what could be done to help survivors. 'I have never witnessed such a gory sight,' he later recalled:

Two men lay on deck with their heads nearly blown to pieces. In the cabin the scene was more heartrending still when I saw six men stretched about anyhow, bleeding and groaning with the agony of their wounds. I had them all removed on board our ship. With all these wounded men on board our floating hospital looked a veritable battlefield.

Indeed, it presented a most pathetic sight. It kept me busy with knife and needle the whole of that day, and it was not until late in the night that I had the satisfaction of seeing them all safe and snug in their cots, as far as circumstances allowed.

The dead and injured arrived home in Hull on a wet and windy Monday watched by crowds of several hundreds. And throughout the Hull fishing community anger rose at the outrage. In London a shouting mob marched on the Russian Embassy and later stoned the building. And in the dusty corridors of Whitehall diplomats met to protest.

In the bustling streets around St Andrew's Dock funeral arrangements were made, leading to an occasion which saw thousands of local

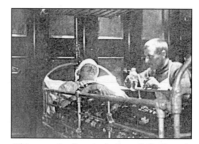

This was the hospital aboard the Joseph and Sarah Miles *in which men from the Russian Outrage were treated.*

Skipper J.W. White, who commanded the mission ship Joseph and Sarah Miles *pictured at the time of the Russian Outrage.*

people turn out to pay their respects. The London based *Black and White* magazine sent a correspondent to the city to cover the events. He reported:

Although the centre of interest after the outrage on the North Sea fishing fleet was quickly removed from Hull to London and is now at Vigo, the sad ceremonies of the funeral brought about a great public demonstration.

The route, which was nearly two miles in length, passed through the populous district of West Hull where fishermen reside, and was crowded with spectators.

Most of the shops were shut and there were many flags at half mast and other tokens of sympathy.

The scene in Ribble Avenue, the residence of Capt George Smith of the Crane *was pathetic and impressive. Capt White, the veteran leader of the Fishermen's Mission, read prayers at the house, then the polished elm coffin bearing the*

Scenes of the homecoming of some of those killed at sea on the Dogger Bank.

legend 'at rest' at the foot and covered with beautiful flowers, was borne from the window to a place in the adjacent square by fishermen clad in their blue jerseys. The band of the local branches of the Order of Buffaloes was drawn up in the square and played Lead Kindly Light. Soon afterwards the coffin containing the body of William Leggott (third hand on the Crane and a native of Yarmouth) arrived from a friend's house and joined the cortege.

Amongst the mourners was Smith's son who was with his father on the Crane at the time of the sad and terrible occurrence.

In the vicinity of the fish docks signs of mourning were particularly notice-able, blinds being drawn and thousands of persons lined the route to the

cemetery. The Mayor and Town Clerk attended the service and hundreds of wreaths were received. The funeral procession was over a mile in length and included the blue jackets from HMS Hearly, *a number of fishermen and representatives of all the Hull public bodies.*

Many pathetic scenes were witnessed at the graveside and the fact that Leggott's mother only heard of his death on the Wednesday morning elicited much sympathy.

Official inquiries were ordered and the incident was investigated by a special inquiry set up in Paris. As a result the Russian Government paid out £65,000 in compensation. Historians would later describe the incident as one of the most tragic mistakes ever made by a naval commander.

Day of disaster

'There is no harder, greyer weather than that of the North Sea. There are no harder Englishmen than deep North Sea men.' – Walter Wood.

Far from home and at sea for up to 10 weeks at a time, returning only to refit and provision, the fishermen of England lived a lonely, frequently dangerous existence on the waters of the North Sea.

In the days when crews put to sea under sail in wooden fishing smacks they usually headed for the Dogger Bank, renowned for its shallow waters and bountiful fish stocks.

Shallow the Dogger may be, but it still presented problems for those daring enough to brave it at its angriest. Its shallowness allows waves no depth to swing and roll in, and as they strike the bank, the vast stretch of sand rising from the sea which helped give the Dogger its full name, they break instead to what has been described as 'an immense cauldron more like a whirlpool than anything else'.

In the later days of steam-driven vessels such conditions became easier to cope with; in the days of the sail-powered fishing smacks they brought danger, and death.

One area of the Dogger infamous for its high mortality rate was known simply as the Cemetery. And it was here, on 6 March 1883, that more than 360 fishermen and boys from east coast ports died in what became known as the Great March Gale.

One writer would later recall: 'The awful visitation destroyed families bodily; fathers and sons went down together and widowed mothers were left penniless in ruined homes. Smacks were overwhelmed bodily and lost with all hands, and the little ships that did escape only reached port after a long, fierce fight and the exercise of wondrous skill and courage by their crews and skippers.'

This is the story of one of them.

He sat cross-legged on the wooden deck of his boat working quietly, a pipe clenched between uneven and blackened teeth. Hands more suited to heavy work, large and calloused, displayed unexpected dexterity and skill as he chivvied away with the large knife on a piece of broken, uneven timber, flotsam thrown on board many weeks before.

The smack floated gently over the stilled waters as he glanced out across the waters of the North Sea, blue in the summer afternoon, the procession of steam ships making their way along the English coast clearly visible in the still, warm air.

Old Ben was a true smacksman, a Dogger warrior of many years now at the end of his working life. As he whittled he thought long and hard about the man who sat quietly beside him, an author come to seek his story. His mind made up, he put down his knife and began to recall the events he had lived through in what had become one of the greatest of all North Sea disasters.

They had sailed from Scarborough, confident and excited at the prospect of a trip which could last for weeks, secure aboard their fine little ketch of 51 tons, christened *Uncle Tom* as she left the stocks some short time earlier.

As they left the harbour, overlooked by the dramatic ruins of the historic castle, the aim of skipper Ben was to get as far out on to the Dogger as possible because he knew after long experience that it was on the bank itself that the best fish could be caught.

Several days later saw them arrive on the area known as the Cemetery, so-called because of the large numbers of men and boys lost there, shooting their trawl and towing it at between two and three knots an hour. But things, Ben suspected, were somehow not quite right:

> *There was something queer and uncanny in the weather, something that I couldn't account for and didn't understand at all. In winter you expect bad weather on the Dogger and you get it; for that matter you sometimes get it all the year round, and I've known a snowstorm out there even in summer time.*

This particular March day conditions just felt strange. The sky was dull, and the sea matched it in dullness. There was little wind, yet seas were beginning to roll around the edge of the bank. Weather experts had predicted a breeze and now it began to come, freshening as they fished on. It was now about 11pm. Darkness enveloped the bank and the boats which fished it.

Ben, an astute skipper, became increasingly concerned, ordering the crew to haul their trawl, fully aware now that something sinister was about to happen. 'I'd scarcely spoken the words when the *Uncle Tom* gave a heavy lurch and the thick trawl warp was snapped just like a piece of thread. There was only one thing to do. The gale had broken on us and even in the darkness I could see the waves tearing towards us. I did all I could to make a run for it.'

Conditions were now volatile and, for the fishing smacks dotted around the Dogger, extremely dangerous. Ben was now committed to making a run for it, fully aware of the dangers as the vessel ran before the wind and the sea, being continually swept by huge waves, her crew expecting that at any second they could be swept overboard or that a single wave would smash the vessel to matchwood.

'She plunged and rolled and pitched in the most awful manner. We were all sodden to the skin in spite of our oilskins and thick clothing, but then I've known us be out for eight and 10 weeks at a time and never dry for a minute, day or night,' said Ben.

Dawn eventually cracked through the heavy skies to show an amazing sight. The shallow waters of the Dogger had become one vast, foaming plain, the wind out of all proportion to the size and fury of the waves. Not far from the *Uncle Tom* a Hull smack fought tenaciously to survive, hammered repeatedly by the heavy seas. 'She seemed to be falling into the trough of an enormous wave. I lost sight of her and looked again, but not a sign of her was left. She'd been smashed bodily by a huge wave and must have been one of the first of the smacks that foundered. I stuck to the tiller and all that day we tore towards Hull.

We were swept and smothered by the seas and everything below was awash or adrift. Immense bodies of water smashed on board but we managed to dodge them. We had to hang on for life but, when there was a chance of doing it, the men jumped below till the seas passed.'

On other smacks men fought only to lose the battle for survival. Men were crushed and maimed or simply swept overboard, never to be seen again. Masts and rigging were unable to stand up to the onslaught of the seas and were carried away. Many small vessels were almost smashed to pieces before they sank.

'In this great gale a man was swept away from the deck of his smack and carried by an enormous sea straight on to the deck of another smack not far off, where he was saved by the crew who clutched him before he could be hurled back. In many cases the huge quantities of water which had tumbled on board burst the companions and got below, filling the smacks and sinking them.'

The *Uncle Tom* continued on her perilous journey, her crew 'perishingly cold' and sodden to the skin. They were unable to eat, their food having been drenched by the seas. And the danger was not over yet. Ben would later recall: 'At last I saw ahead the cliffs down by Flamborough Head and knew that the most dangerous part of the business had to be got through. The only chance of safety was in getting the smack into Bridlington Bay but with such a tremendous run of the sea the chances were equal that in rounding the Head she would be capsized.'

He decided that to try to turn the vessel would be akin to suicide. There was only one thing he could do and that was to await the turn of the tide.

But that did not bring relief. For two days, through four tides, the *Uncle Tom* wallowed off the head. Then – suddenly – he saw his chance 'and I took it like a starving dog snaps a bone.'

The small vessel ran out of the bad weather into the calmer waters of Bridlington Bay, sheltered by the head. And before them they saw the results of the storm... 'a great fleet of ships, many of them crippled. At night they looked like a town lit up.'

It was on a Sunday that they arrived in Hull, amazed to find that fishing smacks completely filled four docks, some of them 'so badly beaten and damaged that it was wonderful that they had escaped at all. It was pitiful to see the battered craft, but even that was easier to look on than to go into the streets where nearly every house had orphans and a widow.'

The *Uncle Tom* was lucky, surviving the ordeal without a scratch. But of the survivors from other vessels there were also the victims. 'There was one young fellow who soon as he got into port said "Look here skipper, let's have my money. I've had enough of the Dogger to last me a lifetime." He was paid off and from that time he never went out to the Dogger Bank again...'

Amy, wonderful Amy

The date was 24 May 1930 – Empire Day. The place was Port Darwin, Australia.

The event – the arrival of a plane called Jason, *piloted by British aviator Amy Johnson, who had completed the flight from England in 19½ days, during which time she was in the air for 126 hours 15 minutes. She completed the journey one day faster than the previous record.*

It was a history making solo journey which fired the imagination of people across the world and made Amy a heroine.

Amy Johnson was born at 154, St George's Road, Hull on 1 July 1903. The eldest daughter of a market salesman in the family firm of Johnson, Knudtzon and Co., she first attended Miss Knowles's school on Anlaby Road in the city and in 1915 transferred to the Boulevard Secondary School.

Amy Johnson became an aviation legend.

A girl of exceptional ability, she became a Bachelor of Arts in 1925 and began work as a secretary with a London firm of solicitors. But to Amy anything mechanical held real fascination, motoring having been one of her hobbies at home in Hull. Her life changed when she was given her first flight in 1928.

After that Amy became fanatical about flying, putting in sufficient hours of solo flight to qualify for a B-pilot's certificate and quickly moving on to gain her full navigation certificate for which 300 hours in the air were needed.

Hull knew little of Amy Johnson until she became an international celebrity following her epic flight to Australia.

DAY 1: The journey began at Croydon Aerodrome in the dim morning light of 5 May 1930, her departure, in the aircraft she christened *Jason,* being seen by only handful of spectators. By 5.50pm that same day she landed at Vienna – a first leg of 700 miles.

DAY 2: Leaving Vienna at 5.50am she set out to reach Constantinople, a distance of 790 miles. Passing over Belgrade and Sofia she completed the journey at 6.10 that evening despite rainstorms over the Balkans, which she admitted were bad 'but not bad enough to frighten me'.

DAY 3: The first mishap of the flight came when just before take-off it was noticed the fuel tank was leaking. Amy was delayed and did not depart until 10.30am for Aleppo, arriving in good time after a 550-mile flight. She immediately set to work and spent three hours overhauling her plane before resting.

DAY 4: 7 May proved eventful and stressful as she headed towards Baghdad. First she became caught in a sandstorm and was forced to land in the desert. She heard dogs barking and was afraid of being found by hostile Arabs, keeping a revolver handy in case of trouble. For two hours she waited until the storm cleared and take-off was possible.

DAY 5: Problems again when on landing at Bundir Abbas she broke the front strut bolt. Again the day's flight was hampered by a sandstorm.

DAY 6: By now being acclaimed as the bravest woman in the world she set off for Karachi, 4,210 miles from London, and went on to Allahabad where she landed on DAY 7 before flying to Calcutta on DAY 8.

DAY 9: From Calcutta Amy ran into problems with heavy rains and strong head winds. Crossing mountains, she was forced to lose height because of bad visibility, eventually following a railway line to reach her destination, but then ran into a ditch on landing, damaging the wings, wheels and propeller.

DAY 12: After two days on the ground for repairs Amy resumed her journey on Friday 16 May heading towards Bangkok. In dreadful weather conditions she completed the trip of 360 miles in 12 hours. It was a bad day, with Amy unable to find a pass through the mountains and becoming completely lost. For three hours she was unable to pick up

International heroine. Amy poses with a fine MG sports car following her amazing flight to Australia. The car was supplied by manufacturer William Morris in recognition of the flight.

any landmarks, but eventually did so and, amid worries about her fuel supply, finally reached her destination.

DAY 13: On 17 May she left for Singapore, reaching Singora on the east coast of the Malay peninsula having covered half the distance and having about 3,000 miles still to go.

DAY 14: Amy arrived at Singapore looking sunburned and cheerful. As the spare propeller fitted at Rangoon had not been specially built she was unable to fly at full speed. A new propeller was fitted by members of the Singapore Flying Club.

DAY 15: Heading towards the Dutch East Indies Amy had an alarming experience when she faced heavy squalls and driving rain while crossing the Java Sea. At times the aircraft was only six feet above the waves. Eventually she reached safety, landing in a rice field and slightly damaging the plane. The rents in the wings were soon repaired, however, and she was able to leave in a reasonably short time.

DAY 16: A long day in which the strain began to show, but Amy pulled herself together to arrive safely at Sourabaya.

DAY 17: Grounded, Amy waited restlessly for repairs to a defective magneto. Time was now against her.

DAY 18: *Jason* was in the air before 5am and in excellent spirits Amy departed a few hours later sending out a message that all was well. But then came silence and for 24

Safely back home Amy Johnson poses for the camera with her father, mother and sisters at a get-together in the Grosvenor Hotel, London.

hours there was no news. Eventually, though, the message came through – she was down and safe in a remote village on Timor. There were problems with fuel, but these were overcome and Amy prepared for take-off. She would later recall: 'As I opened up the throttle the trees of the jungle rushed nearer... I am certain that my wheels touched the tree-tops as I felt *Jason* give a lurch...' From there she progressed to the small town of Atamboea to overhaul her engine.

DAY 19: In the jungle town Amy worked under the blazing sun for her final journey, one which was to make her internationally famous. Petrol was available but only in rusty cans and had to be filtered before it could be pumped into the aircraft tanks. Amy would say later: 'As for oil, by good fortune I had a spare gallon with me... It was long after dark before I finished work.'

DAY 20: Saturday 24 May and a cheerful start for the last leg of the journey when Shell announced that an oil tanker had been instructed to stand by on her course on the way to Darwin. It was a welcome boost. It was a reasonably easy journey, Amy arriving in Australia to a massive welcome. Among the messages of congratulations was one from the King of England.

From there Amy became an international celebrity, achieving other amazing flying feats. But the story of the greatest woman flyer of all time ended in tragedy. Amy died in the Thames Estuary on 5 January 1941 – a tragedy that left a mystery which remains to this day... was there a mystery passenger flying with her? And if so, who was he?

Skipper who left men to die

The skipper stood to attention as the destroyer captain looked him slowly up and down, his brow furrowed, his concentration intense.

'What is the name of your vessel?' the German demanded.

'King Stephen.'

'King Stephen, eh. Then you will be shot.'

That – thankfully for Skipper Tom Collins and his crew following an encounter with the German Navy in the North Sea during the height of World War One – did not happen.

But the captain's words reflected the hatred of his countrymen for that particular trawler, which achieved notoriety in a dramatic tale of the sea which saw 19 Germans die and a Grimsby skipper killed by fright...

Grimsby, January 1916

It was clear, bright day with just a hint of wind whispering down the Humber. On the lines of trawlers moored in the fish dock men worked on nets and laughed and joked as they prepared their vessels for sea. As high tide came several slipped through the lock head and into the river. Among them was GY 174, *King Stephen*.

Gently she entered the estuary, turned to starboard and under the expert guidance of Skipper William Martin began her journey to the North Sea fishing grounds. Carefully the skipper, a confident, well respected fisherman, checked his charts and the compass bearing as he began to relax, aware only of the shrill of the wind through the ill-fitting door.

Below, in their cabin, the crew reflected on their time ashore in the pubs around the fish dock. The days ahead would be hard, long days of intense effort. They rested now. But not for long.

The North Sea, 2 February 1916

Fishing was going well and the catches were reasonable. William Martin was pleased with what he saw and in particular with his crew. Good men, loyal and hard working. Some had been with him for many trips.

In the early hours of the morning the darkness was intense, heavy cloud obliterating both the moon and the stars. They were alone and at peace with nature. Then he saw it not too far away from them, a light, or what appeared to be a light. Alert now, the skipper peered into the gloom, moving out on to the deck to try to gain a better view.

There it was again, yes it was a light. He alerted the crew, ordered the nets to be hauled and as soon as that operation was completed changed course, the crew gathered on the deck trying to make out where the light was coming from.

Suddenly in the approaching dimness of dawn they saw the upperworks of a zeppelin, towering above the waves, the cabin structure now vanished from view. George Denny, mate of the *King Stephen*, takes up the story:

'When we got near enough to make it out clearly I saw about eight men on top of the ship and they were shouting and waving to us. The light was getting clear by the time we got to within hailing distance and we could see that a great part of the ship was under water.

'I should think that there would be 50 feet of the fore part of the envelope above water; in fact the top of it was as high as our masthead and we had to go close up to it to hear what the men were shouting.

'I saw a lot more men come on top through a scuttle hatch. I counted 18 of them and one man, who had brass buttons on his uniform, appeared to be the commander. They all had lifelines attached to them from the hatchway and they were shouting to us in broken English "save us, save us, we give you much gold. Take us off!"'

The commander of the zeppelin, a young man wearing the Iron Cross and two other decorations, spoke politely and in good English as he put his case. But Martin was a tough man, quick to realise the dangers of the situation.

'I had all my men safe and sound and I was determined to take no risks. I knew what the Germans had done to my class in the North Sea and besides, the fact that zeppelin crews were dropping bombs on houses and killing women and children didn't appeal to me.'

The huge size of the zeppelins is clearly shown in this picture from a museum in Denmark.

For Skipper Martin the situation posed a massive dilemma. All he and his crew could do was stare into the gloom, aghast. The problem was serious, of that there was no doubt. And the options were simple – leave the Germans where they were or rescue them and face the prospect of seeing the *King Stephen* taken over and sailed to Germany. In numbers the Germans were definitely superior. They also had guns, whereas the fishermen carried only sticks.

Martin would later recall: 'After considering the pros and cons we agreed that if we lowered a boat and sent some of the crew to the zeppelin they would at once be secured and kept prisoners until we did as the Germans wished which would probably be that in the end we should have them take charge of the ship if they came on board or if we refused to fetch them off they would carry our boat and crew down with them.

'Our safety was certain where we were, but our liberty once they boarded us wasn't worth a penny so I told the commander plainly that nothing he could say would induce me to rescue them.'

It was a decision which received full support from mate Denny, who said:

'They could easily have overpowered us and taken our ship to Germany with us as prisoners, that is if they did not pitch us overboard first.

'So he shouted to them that he could not take them off and they all started shouting and saying they would not touch us if only we saved them. They screeched for us to save them but the skipper did right when he said he could not take them.

'What would their Kaiser say to them if he got to know that nine of us chaps had been able to overpower 25 of them and bring them prisoners to Grimsby?'

In making his decision Skipper Martin knew he was condemning the Germans to death. There were no other vessels in the vicinity. The zeppelin was obviously doomed and sinking. They had no lifeboats. His decision was a courageous one, taken in the best interests of his own crew. But it was one which would trigger furious debate and anger for years to follow. To leave men to die was against every tradition of the sea. But Martin's mind was made up. His own ship and his crew's safety were of paramount importance. Slowly the *King Stephen* began to inch away from the airship.

'It was no use adding to the agony or aggravating ourselves for, after all, it wasn't a nice feeling to leave 18 men to drown even if they were your enemies and richly deserving their fate. I rang the telegraph to slow ahead and we began to sheer off.

'Directly the commander saw what we were doing and that there was no chance of being rescued he set up a howl and the others set up a howl. Their rage was awful. Shaking their fists in despair they kept shouting "Gott strafe England" and they shouted again and again as long as we were in hearing. If half what (the commander) promised had been true I should have been rich for life but there are times when common sense is worth more than all the gold in the world and this was one of them.'

And so they left her and her crew, marooned and without hope. There were no immediate signs that the zeppelin would sink quickly, for she still had a vast amount of gas within her. But by now the wind was freshening, dead calm sea beginning to roll and to pitch. Pulled down by the weight of its car, now ever deeper below the surface, the frame would soon begin to break apart as the seas smashed against it.

In those last moments men prayed, cursed and reflected on their lives and on their fate. Two managed to scrawl messages on to slips of paper and place them into a bottle which two months later would be washed ashore and discovered. One would read: 'Our last hour is at hand…' The other would carry a more moving message: 'My greetings to my wife and child. An English trawler was here and refused to take us on board. She was the *King Stephen* and she hailed from Grimsby…'

From Grimsby news of the incident spread fast, making Skipper Martin a hero in Britain and a war criminal in Germany. One British newspaper, coming down in support of the skipper's actions, commented: 'With remarkable blindness to the inhumanities of their own people and with sublime hypocrisy the German newspapers angrily and roundly condemn the action of the master and crew of the Grimsby vessel. The impudent effrontery of the German tirade is only fully realised when it is remembered that this very zeppelin crew, not long before had been guilty of bombing a British steamer without making any attempt to rescue the crew of the ship, most of whom lost their lives…'

And letters flooded in both to the press and Skipper Martin. Almost all of them supported him, one which appeared in the *Grimsby Evening Telegraph* ably summing up the overall feeling: 'As an Englishman I must congratulate you for the manner in which you treated those cowardly, miserable wretches in leaving them to their fate, which was far too good for them. Had you attempted to rescue them I, and thousands more, would say you ought to have been shot...'

But for Skipper Martin the ordeal was to prove too much. The affair preyed on his mind and about 11 months after the incident he collapsed and died. Some claimed he believed he had been poisoned for he had received death threats from Germans still living in England and Wales. When he became ill after smoking a cigarette which had been sent to him in a packet through the post he became ever more convinced that it had contained poison. But a doctor who examined him said the cause was much more simple: 'He died from sheer fright.'

As for the *King Stephen*, she carried on putting out to sea but in a different role. After making international headlines the trawler, owned by the Consolidated Steam Fishing Company, was requisitioned by the Admiralty and converted to a decoy ship.

The aim of such vessels – they were known as Q-ships – was to look innocent, while packing a punch, being fitted with concealed armament, strengthening and a pigeon loft.

But although this work was carried out the men at the Admiralty, for reasons best known to themselves, failed to change her name. So when, under the command of Tom Phillips, of Lowestoft, an RNR 'special service' volunteer who had already sunk one German submarine, she headed into the North Sea to act as U-boat bait, the scene was set for a second drama.

A first U-boat was spotted two miles away from the *King Stephen,* which gave chase and fired six rounds, revealing the true nature of her mission.

But when searching for a German naval patrol boat Phillips found himself face-to-face with the German High Seas Fleet returning from a bombardment of Lowestoft and Yarmouth. It was an encounter from which he had no chance of successfully escaping.

His vessel was sunk and the crew were taken prisoner, being stoned by a mob when they were taken ashore. Kept prisoner until the end of the war, one of them was permanently disabled by the blow he received from the rifle wielded by a German guard.

The crew of the stranded L-19 are seen on top of the zeppelin as the Grimsby trawler King Stephen *sails away after her skipper decided that to rescue the Germans would put his crew in danger.*

True men of courage

The colours of the East Yorkshire Regiment.

They were heroes among heroes, men whose bravery earned them the highest award for gallantry their country could offer – the Victoria Cross. Four serving soldiers from the East Yorkshire Regiment earned the nation's respect for their supreme efforts during World War One. These are their stories.

No.19384 Pte George William Chafer VC (1st Battalion, East Yorkshire Regiment)

Although severely wounded in three places Chafer won the regiment's first VC in the war. The official citation in the *London Gazette* said: 'East of Meaulte, France, June 3/4 1916. For most conspicuous bravery. During a very heavy hostile bombardment and attack upon our trenches a man carrying an important written message to his company commander was half buried and rendered unconscious by a shell. Private Chafer, at once grasping the situation, on his own initiative took the message from the man's pocket and, although severely wounded in three places, ran along the ruined parapet under heavy shell and machine-gun fire and just succeeded in delivering it before he collapsed from the effects of his wounds. He displayed great initiative and a splendid devotion to duty at a crucial moment.'

The story was later recorded in a history of the regiment which was published in 1928 and which gave a much more dramatic account of the incident: 'The scene was terrible. Our trench had been almost levelled by enfilade shell fire and enemy trench mortars. It was being swept by deadly machine-gun fire and was poisoned by gas fumes.

'Chafer was lying seriously wounded in hand and leg, bruised and dazed by the concussion, choking and blinded by gas, when he saw a man coming along with a written message.

Pte George William Chafer VC.

'Another shell burst and partially buried this orderly who shouted: "Someone take this message for the captain." There was no one within hearing but Chafer. Only dead and mortally wounded men were in sight. Nine hundred and ninety-nine men out of a thousand would have said "I can't do anything. I have done my bit. Now I lie low in what cover I've got. The message can't be delivered." Not so Chafer. His attitude was not "I can't," but "I will try, at all costs it must be done."

'He took the message from the soldier and as the trench had been knocked in so badly, crawled on to the parapet in spite of excruciating pain. There were big shells, small shells, bullets from machine guns and rifles raining around and how he came through without further injury is a miracle.

'The first living occupant of our trench whom Chafer reached was a corporal. The latter could hardly believe his eyes when he saw someone, wearing a gas helmet, his left hand shot through and bleeding profusely yet clutching his rifle, dragging himself painfully along the parapet with one leg torn by shell wounds, crying all the time "A message for the captain." After handing it over, Chafer collapsed.'

No.12/21 Pte John Cunningham VC (12th (S) Battalion, East Yorkshire Regiment)

The date was 13 November 1916. In the muddy hell that was the front line trenches of France Pte Cunningham became a hero.

The official citation published in the *London Gazette* would record that he received the highest award for 'for most conspicuous bravery and resource during operations. Pte

Cunningham proceeded with a bombing section up a communication trench. Much opposition was encountered and the rest of the section became casualties.

'Collecting all the bombs from the casualties, this gallant soldier went on alone. Having expended all his bombs, he then returned for a fresh supply and again proceeded to the communication trench, where he met a party of 10 of the enemy. These he killed and cleared the trench up to the enemy line. His conduct throughout the day was magnificent.'

Pte John Cunningham VC.

The 12th Battalion narrative of that day gives little insight into the incident which earned one of it members the highest award of all for bravery. It recorded: 'The trenches had been so blown about that it was impossible to make them really defensive. The Germans counter-attacked in force, twice during the day from the left, but were annihilated by our Lewis guns. The whole day was spent in fighting small parties, bombers and snipers. In the evening, as there was a danger of being surrounded, it was decided to withdraw, the last party retiring about 8.45pm.'

And that is that. The narrative makes no mention of Pte Cunningham or the heroic hand-to-hand fighting that earned him the VC and his regiment battlefield glory.

2nd Lt John Harrison MC VC (11th (S) Battalion, East Yorkshire Regiment)

The barrage was relentless, the noise deafening and dust, smoke and darkness added to the dreadful atmosphere. This was Oppy Wood. The date was 3 May 1917 and the 11th East Yorkshires were facing a screen of fire which poured from the German front line.

Raked by machine gun fire from enemy posts in the wood, and subjected to rifle fire

Lt John Harrison MC, VC.

from the front line trenches, the Yorkshiremen fought back, managing to edge forward despite the fire which raked across the desolation of the battleground.

It was a courageous, but futile attempt to win a few yards of wasteland. Out in No Man's Land and still under heavy enemy fire officers managed to re-form their men and again led them forward and were again repulsed. But it was to take more than the German front line to stop John Harrison.

The leader of a solitary platoon, he went on to the attack again, 'rallying his men with words of confidence' as he led them forward. It was a dangerous, suicidal manoeuvre, one in which three belts of thick barbed wire had to be negotiated. But Harrison knew that on the extreme southern point of Oppy Wood a German machine gun was playing havoc among the platoons, scything down men and making British progress impossible.

A report of the incident said: 'Ordering his men to take shelter in shell holes, but to keep the machine gun under continuous rifle grenade fire, Harrison, carrying a Mills bomb in his hand, attempted to rush the gun single-handed.

'He had almost reached the gun and had just hurled his bomb at the German crew when his men saw him fall, face downwards. But he had accomplished his self imposed task – the machine gun never fired again. For this very gallant deed 2nd Lt Harrison was awarded the Victoria Cross and no man deserved it more. He had given his life to save others.'

Lt Harrison was reported missing, believed killed.

No.18474 Sgt Harold Jackson VC (7th (S) Battalion, East Yorkshire Regiment)

For three days the bombardment continued, an incessant onslaught of noise, explosion and death. The 7th East Yorkshires held on gallantly, trapped in their trenches near Hermies, France, as the Germans threw everything at them. In one bombardment alone shells rained down for six hours, gas attacks adding to the devastation of high explosive.

As dawn broke on 22 March 1918, men prepared for yet another attack. They knew it was coming, but not when, and they feared its intensity. Already in the cold light of dawn a preparatory barrage of the front line had opened.

Harold Jackson knew, as did every man serving with him, that this was the prelude to an attack of exceptional intensity. He was tired, chilled, hungry – and yet resolute, convinced that they could turn the tide.

As daybreak came he volunteered to leave the trench in which they had spent a cold, sleepless and cheerless night amid the stench of decay and death, the cries of the injured, some untended, many dying, eerie in the darkness.

Jackson could stand the waiting no longer, He needed action. And he volunteered for daylight patrol. It was an act of great bravery. He crept out of the trench, inching his way forward, slowly and carefully picking his way across the morass of mud and bodies towards the enemy line, watching every movement, checking every position, careful to remember every movement, every clue.

His information, he was later told, was of great value. But it did not allow the British to prevent a renewed attack penetrating the battalion's trenches. That was something Jackson would not tolerate, whatever the danger to himself. An account of the action would later reveal the full dramatic story:

'Sgt Jackson held an impromptu bombing stop and by his vigorous offensive forced the Germans to retire. Later he stalked an enemy machine gun which was enfilading the battalion's trenches and, single-handed, hurled Mills bombs and put a gun definitely out of action, killing or wounding the entire crew.'

And, it would be recorded 'for seven days he fought with magnificent gallantry during the rearguard actions'.

An official recommendation for him to be awarded the VC ended: 'On 31 March at Bouzincourt, he took command of his company after all his officers had become casualties, led them to the attack with splendid bravery and initiative and withdrew when ordered to do so under heavy fire. And took up a good new defensive position.

Sgt Harold Jackson VC.

'He afterwards repeatedly went out into the open and brought back badly wounded men under a murderous enemy fire. His wonderful coolness and devotion to duty under the most trying conditions has set the highest example to everyone.'

But Sgt Jackson did not survive the war. His citation in the *London Gazette* records simply that he was killed in action.

King of the cowboys

Along the uneven boardwalk they made their way towards the broken down shack at the end of a row of similarly dilapidated buildings. On the street dust flurries spiralled skywards, encouraged by the hot desert wind.

The building they entered stood on the corner of Second and Utah streets in the bustling Texas town of El Paso and was known to men working the ranges across a vast area simply as Tillie Howard's after the tough and blowsy woman who ran the establishment.

What followed would later be epitomised in a hundred Hollywood movies. Shots were fired and men were killed. One received bullets in the head, another was hit twice in the leg. The gunman who caused this mayhem was shot too, receiving a chest wound from which he would die after staggering to a nearby saloon.

The shoot-out was witnessed by a man known to all who took part although he had no role to play in the drama. He was Frank Collinson, an East Yorkshire man who was to make a name for himself thousands of miles away from his native county, a king of the cowboys who would live to become a famous figure in Wild West folklore...

The great minster bells boomed out their dignified message over the red pantiled rooftops of the surrounding houses and across the town itself, the sound echoing down alleyways and roads and, carried by the wind, becoming lost in the morning mist as it touched the edge of the great open space on the western side of Beverley.

It was a reassuring sound, a familiar sound to all who lived there, this summons to Sunday service, a comfortable part of town life in a historic settlement formed around that magnificent tribute to Gothic architecture which seemed as old as time itself.

In the comfort of his bed Walter James Collinson did not hear the bell which awakened Beverley to its prayers that particular Sunday morning. He lay still, although wide awake, oblivious to his surroundings but deep in thought.

His young mind wandered to what he believed the great plains of America were like, their vast, bleak landscapes littered with great herds of buffalo, their mountains places of danger from warlike Indians.

That day would again see him out by the gate, a home-made lariat in his hand as he tried in vain to lasso the post. And later he would return to the house to read once more the letter from Captain Story, a relative of his mother's who lived in Texas. He was a man with a tale to tell and he recounted it well, having fought in the Battle of San Jacinto, owned a wagon yard in San Antonio and held an interest in a stage line.

He was a man who fascinated Walter – more generally known as Frank – who in his 'typical middle-class refined home' in Yorkshire let his imagination of life in the Wild West run free. Many years later Collinson would write: 'My parents were intelligent and sympathetic... when I persisted day after day talking about Texas and my desire to become a cowboy my parents also caught the vision.'

And with their blessing, not to mention money for his fare, Frank Collinson found himself on the dockside at Liverpool one September day in 1872, waving goodbye to his brother who had accompanied him as he boarded the *San Marcos*, a Black Star Line steamship bound for Galveston. The vessel was a new one and this was her maiden voyage. She carried six passengers, of whom Frank was the youngest. It was a momentous moment for the 17-year-old.

Collinson wrote: 'My brother told me "good-bye" and got off. The sailors were ready to haul in the ropes, but most of the stokers, a tough bunch from Liverpool, were late and showed up just about sailing time. They were half drunk and then went down to their quarters to have another jug. Something must have happened because they were soon back on deck and trying to get off.

'The skipper had raised the gangplank and the excitement began. The engineers and officers drove the stokers below with clubs and the captain gave the tugboat the signal to start down the Mersey...'

Frank Collinson did not take long to adapt to life as a cowboy. By the age of 21 he had seen – and done – things he had dreamed of for years.

But he was a young man with ambition and soon decided that wages of only 40 dollars a month did not go far and life on trail drives was not really exciting enough. It was then he decided to join a band of men who were to change for ever the look of the American West. The cowboy from Yorkshire bought himself a heavy calibre gun and went off to join the buffalo hunters, teaming up with a fugitive from the law who had killed several men in New Mexico.

His real name was Wilson, but he was best known as Jim White. He found Texas an ideal place to hide from the lawmen who sought him. He was, said Collinson, 'a tough hombre', but one he acknowledged was the most outstanding hunter and frontiersman he would ever meet...

It was a chance conversation between strangers. One was a rancher, a quite prosperous young man, the other a United States Customs official. The official, inquisitive and knowledgeable, was keen to hear the rancher's tales of life on the range. And also those of the great days of the buffalo hunt.

'Have you ever heard of a hunter called Collinson?' he asked.

'Yeah, I sure have. Why do you ask?'

'It was amazing. I once counted over 100 buffalo killed on one stand south of the Red River and was told Collinson had killed them.'

'I am that man,' was the reply.

In fact Collinson had killed more than that in a single stand, his best ever total being 121 animals felled with just over 300 shots from a Sharps 45-calibre 15-pound gun. It was a hard life for the East Yorkshireman but he loved it, even though at times the realities of the killing fields were not for the squeamish, as he would later recall:

...I have killed and seen killed thousands of buffalo cows. They were skinned and their calves left to starve to death or be killed by the wolves and coyotes. These little calves were lying by the dead cows. We had to keep driving them away while skinning the cows. I saw some of them trying to suck the cows. After the mothers were skinned and the hides were in the wagon, the calves followed. They were gone next morning, gone back to where they had sucked the last time. Either to starve to death or to be killed by the wolves...

To many the buffalo hunters were the dregs of the border towns and railroad camps, but Collinson believed otherwise. 'There were many well educated and cultured men who hunted buffalo... the hunters I knew were real men, good average citizens trying to make a living.'

Among them was Montie Long, with whom Collinson had a memorable experience while resting up at Fort Sumner, New Mexico. Montie was camped up, spending his time drinking and gambling. Nearby was a store run by an elderly couple who were afraid of the hunter, especially when he was drunk and shooting his gun into the trees.

Collinson takes up the story: 'One evening Montie walked to the store and said "open up old man or I'll shoot inside". There was no immediate answer and Montie kept his word. His bullet hit a 25-pound keg of gunpowder. It exploded with a terrific noise, taking the roof off the store.

'I helped get the old couple out. The woman was injured by falling poles and dirt, but she recovered. Montie paid to have the roof repaired and remarked that you could not kill folks like them...'

The hunter led a mean existence and there were frequently moments of danger posed by Indians fighting to retain their traditional territorial rights. In several encounters with the tribes Collinson saw men and women die in vicious fighting. He, too, was involved in skirmishes with Indians, among them the Battle at Yellow House Draw, a dramatic confrontation which became known as 'the scalp hunt...'

For centuries they had ruled the plains, free men fighting nature for their very existence. The great herds of buffalo provided them with the basic essentials of food and clothing, the beasts falling to their spears and arrows in culls which required amazing dexterity, horsemanship and courage. But then came the white man.

As the settlers poured into America from the east and then began to journey across the vast open spaces of its interior, they brought with them a threat to a way of life which had, it seemed, existed for ever. The herds fell to the guns of the hunters. Railroads were built across land which had been fought over and protected. And for the proud tribes who had inhabited this wild and barren place came another threat – that of life restricted to reservations created by the white man.

For the proud braves of the Comanche and Kiowa tribes the prospect was demeaning and unacceptable. They had seen their lands invaded, their lifestyles ruined. But they were determined they would not let it end without a fight. On the plains the tribes were supposed to have been resettled on the Fort Sill Reservation, but small raiding parties kept returning to their traditional hunting grounds for food and to carry out revenge attacks on the strangers who had forced them into submission. In particular they looked upon the rising number of white buffalo hunters as prime targets, and when opportunity knocked they were swift to strike, raiding camps and setting them on fire, slashing hides and even killing.

It was a situation which the white settlers decided could not be tolerated and in March 1877 a group of hunters gathered at a trading post to see what could be done. There was wide acceptance that action was needed against the 'red devils' and agreement was reached that a posse of about 50 hunters, led by Spotted Jack who was part Indian, part Negro and who had lived for some time with the Comanches, would set out.

Collinson would later write: 'Many of the men went along for the very love of the sport of getting a scalp and I am sure that I belonged to that class.'

With some men riding on five heavily loaded wagons and about 30 on horseback the party set out on the last day of March, the hunters in high spirits as most had drunk to their success before leaving. Leading them was Spotted Jack, said to be a fine scout, a good shot and a great whisky drinker, and he pondered on a journey that he knew would take them 150 miles on to the plains.

As confrontation neared excitement built up. 'It was like a picnic. The men felt the big fight would soon be coming off and celebrated accordingly. They more they drank the more scalps they envisioned as souvenirs,' said Collinson.

Two nights into their mission scouts reported Indian tracks leading to Yellow House Draw, a dried-up river bed. It was there that Spotted Jack, riding well ahead of the party, saw that Indians had set up camp. For the hunters this was good news indeed. They cleaned their guns, and prepared for action. Whisky flowed late into the night.

The attack came around dawn as the Comanches were awakening. '...We could see the Indian tipis ahead of us and this was the signal to charge. Some men left their horses and ran up the side of the draw and began to shoot over the top of the men still on horseback.

'We were about a hundred yards from the Indian camp and the bullets were coming thick and fast. We could see no Indians but they were evidently shooting at us from behind the tipis. Spotted Jack was the first to fall. He was a dead hombre...'

Another hunter fell from his horse critically wounded and others were hit in the hail of bullets. It was then that Jim Campbell, a Scots hunter with a fearsome reputation in a fight, who had been chosen to lead the party, intervened, calling his men back and then ordering half of them to return to Yellow House Draw, the rest remaining further back in case of a Comanche counter attack.

'We could see no Indians but we rose back anyway shooting at tipis. This time there were no answering shots. We continued forward and found the Indians gone, the tipis full of holes and a few dead horses on the ground.

'Far up the west draw we could see a faint cloud of dust left by the fleeing Indians. We burned the tipis and rode back to Campbell... there was not a scalp in the bunch to show for our trouble.

'The body of Spotted Jack was picked out of the dust and carried to a wagon. Another wounded man was also lifted to a wagon and made as comfortable as possible but he had been shot through the stomach and died two days later...'

The battle was the first of several waged against the Comanches by buffalo hunters. And from Collinson it brought the view that they had not had the opportunity to be very heroic. 'If our men had been sober and properly led we could have whipped half the Comanche tribe. But who could handle 30 or 40 half-drunk buffalo hunters? We got licked and well licked.'

Collinson was to have another skirmish with the Comanches, again at Yellow House Draw. But it was the end of an era in the west. The buffalo were now few and those who hunted them turned to other ways of making a living. For the Yorkshireman the future now lay elsewhere...

The wages, so the story went, were good. But the work was both dangerous and of dubious legality. With the buffalo gone an unemployed Frank Collinson decided on a new career, heading for the Pecos River where he was told good money could be earned for sharpshooters willing to join the cattle king John Chisum in the Lincoln County war.

It was a matter he raised at a meeting with Chisum's brother Pitser, who told him the story was untrue. Contrary to popular belief his brother was not hiring a highly paid army. But a friend of his was looking for cattlemen to drive 8,000 head from Fort Sumner, New Mexico, to Texas. It was a challenge Collinson could not resist and he accepted without hesitation, moving on to John Chisum's ranch to begin his journey. It was there he was to meet one of the west's most notorious villains – Billy the Kid. It happened one evening when a group of men rode up and turned their horses loose near the Pecos River.

'One of them was a slim boyish fellow. He was supposed to be 18 but looked older when you saw him closely. He was sunburned and not much to look at. Everything he had on would not have sold for five dollars – an old black slouch hat; worn out pants and boots, spurs, shirt and vest; a black cotton handkerchief tied loosely around his neck,

ever ready Colt double action .41 pistol around him and in easy reach, an old style .44 rim fire, brass-jawed Winchester.

'I should say he was about five feet seven inches tall and weighed perhaps 135 pounds. He had no chin, no shoulders and his hands and feet were small. He needed a haircut. He had a pair of grey-clear eyes that never stopped looking around...'

Collinson remained at the ranch for several weeks with little to do. While they were still rounding up cattle for the drive rumours began to grow of a threat to the Chisum empire from a group known as the Seven Rivers Outfit. Chisum, not a man to take threats likely, decided to take action of his own.

'All hands were urged to

Billy the Kid.

get to the ranch as fast as possible. I ran to the wagon and took out my Sharps .45 from where it had been rolled in a blanket and joined the rest of the Chisum cowboys as they headed out on for Spring River.

'The Kid and his party were there when we got there and the Seven Rivers Outfit had cleared out leaving a trail of dust. I was disappointed there was no gun battle. The big fight took place at Lincoln Plaza a few days later.'

Collinson hit the trail again, spending many years travelling the west and – in 1887 – marrying a Scots girl, Jessamin Brammer- in Lamar, Colorado. He witnessed an era the like of which will never be seen again, one of lawlessness and rough justice, high adventure and discovery.

But the pioneering spirit of the Old West was dying. Times were changing and a way of life that he had loved was soon to vanish. Collinson, the trail driver, buffalo hunter, Indian fighter and cattleman settled down and raised a family, at one point going into business, buying a silver mine in Mexico from which, it is said, he made a great deal of money.

And then he became a writer, his memories of the west being avidly read by subscribers to Ranch Romances *magazine and today regarded as among the most authentic accounts of that period.*

Frank Collinson, a tall, heavy-set man easily identifiable by his mustache, which measured 15 inches from tip to tip, died at the age of 87 in 1943. He is buried in Clarendon, Texas.

Note: Collinson's writings, originally published in *Ranch Romances* magazine, have been re-published by the University of Oklahoma Press under the title *Life in the Saddle*.

Disaster in the
North Atlantic

It was one of the great tragedies of the 20th century. The loss of the liner Titanic *has for decades been a story which has fascinated millions.*

Among those involved in the running of the ship on its ill-fated maiden voyage was a 28-year-old Hull man. This is his story...

As the film many years later would so dramatically recall, it was a night to remember. And for Joseph Groves Boxhall it was one which would haunt him for the rest of his life – and eventually lead to his ashes being scattered over the wild Atlantic Ocean 55 years after the terrible night which saw the loss of the *Titanic*.

Joseph Boxhall was born of a seafaring family on 23 March 1884 and the sea was the only career he seemed to be interested in. Indeed, by the time he first boarded *Titanic* in Belfast shortly before her sea trials on 2 April 1912 he had already been sailing for 13 years, serving an apprenticeship with the Liverpool firm of William Thomas, but later returning to Hull to take up a post with the Wilson Line. He was regarded as an outstanding navigator.

It was not long before he passed his master's certificate, which led to him joining the White Star Line, where he served for five years before being appointed to the crew of the biggest, most luxurious passenger liner ever to be built.

It was a posting that many seamen could only have dreamed of, but Boxhall's skills stood him in good stead. Captain Edward Smith was so confident of his young officer's ability that he assigned Boxhall the responsibility of keeping the vessel's charts up to date. It was a big responsibility for a young man who earned just £9 a month.

At 11.40pm on the night of 4 April 1912, as *Titanic* made her way sedately across a silent and calm ocean, Fourth Officer Boxhall strode confidently on to the bridge, taking up his position and checking their course. Suddenly the orderly calm was shattered by the clanging of the warning bell being sounded in the crow's nest, signalling the presence of icebergs. Boxhall, who would later recall hearing orders called out by the first officer to the quartermaster, was aware of a collision. It appeared minor. There was, he and others believed at that moment, nothing to worry about.

Boxhall made his way to the bridge to find Captain Smith and the sixth officer in deep conversation as they debated what should be done. Boxhall was dispatched immediately to inspect the ship, but could see no damage. During his tour of inspection he was handed a large piece of ice by one of the passengers.

The inspection took about 15 minutes and then he returned to the bridge where he was ordered to find a carpenter to sound the ship. As he set out on his mission came word that the forward compartments were filling with water – and fast.

The scene was set for one of the greatest sea dramas of all time.

As officer in charge of navigation Boxhall had to calculate *Titanic's* position. Once he had done so Captain Smith went to the wireless room and asked for a call for assistance to be sent out. Boxhall knew now that *Titanic* was doomed. Outside, on the decks, in the staterooms and cabins, panic was starting to set in among the passengers, as the word swept through the ship that she was taking in water.

The phone rang and Boxhall grabbed it, hearing the voice of Quartermaster George Rowe, who reported seeing a lifeboat in the water, a fact which caused Boxhall some surprise as he had not ordered any of the boats to be launched. His mind racing, he ordered Rowe to fetch distress rockets to the bridge.

Things were growing steadily worse. By 12.45am Boxhall and Rowe started to fire rockets from the bridge. Boxhall, believing he could see a ship in the distance – probably 10 miles away he estimated – tried to make contact with it through a Morse lamp. It was a futile attempt.

As passengers were prepared to abandon ship, Boxhall was in charge of lifeboat No.2 which was lowered at 1.45am from the vessel's port side. It carried only 18 people, although it had a capacity to take 40.

Slowly, but steadily, the boat inched away from the stricken liner and, in stunned silence, the passengers looked on helplessly as slowly, almost sedately, the 'unsinkable' *Titanic's* stern rose ever higher above the sea before crashing back downwards to vanish for ever.

Devastated and distressed, Boxhall managed to maintain control over his emotions, asking the women on his boat if they believed he should return to the scene to help people swimming in the freezing water. They said they did not wish to return, fearing their boat would be swamped with panic-stricken survivors.

And so they drifted, cold, shocked and stunned into silence, with Boxhall still vainly trying to summon help by firing green flares into the inky black night sky. Relief finally came at around 4am when the *Carpathia* was sighted on the horizon, Boxhall setting off a final flare to guide the rescue vessel towards them.

He would later tell Captain Rostron, of the *Carpathia*: '...Hundreds and hundreds, perhaps a thousand or more... my God, sir they've gone down with her. They couldn't live in this cold water.'

Boxhall was called on to give evidence of the events of that fateful night at the two inquiries into the disaster. He then returned to his seagoing career, becoming first officer on Cunard White Star's *Aquitania* in the 1930s. Later he was given command but he left the sea in 1940.

Eighteen years later he was appointed technical director for the feature film *A Night to Remember*.

Joseph Boxhall died in April 1967 at the age of 83. Two months later his ashes were cast on the cold, bleak waters of the Atlantic at the exact position he had calculated Titanic *to be in when she sank 55 years earlier.*

Back from the dead

For over 100 years the men who sailed the Humber fishing fleets courted death. Thousands were injured or lost their lives in what was unquestionably the most dangerous job of all.

They were the unsung heroes of the British working class, men who faced the very worst that nature could throw at them as part of their daily working lives. It was a job which required stamina, determination and, above all, high courage.

From the outset fishing brought its own stories of adventure and heroism.

Here we go back to November 1889 and join the crew of the Grimsby fishing vessel Sando on a trip which would take them to the brink of death in a five-month ordeal that must rank as one of the most amazing stories ever faced by the hunters of the deep...

Grimsby was thriving. And the reason why lay in its bustling fishing dock. Trawling was big business and entrepreneurs were quick to catch on to the fact. By the end of the 1880s there were around 800 vessels sailing from the port and collectively they made almost 19,000 voyages a year.

For George Clifford the trip he had just completed was, he confidently expected, to be the last of 1889. It was November, the weather was poor and 29-year-old George had a burning desire to be home with his family for Christmas and probably beyond. It was, he argued, a long time since he had been able to enjoy such a luxury.

It was a knock on the door which changed his mind – and his life. On the step was a ship's husband, a man he had known for many years. The conversation was brief and to the point.

'George, we want a man for the *Sando*. Will you do a trip in her for us?'

'No, I'm having a trip ashore.'

The man pressed him hard. 'Come on, George, do us a favour.'

But the deckhand was adamant and stood his ground. 'No. You'll have to get someone else.'

'OK, I'll make you an offer. I will give you half a sovereign, a pound of tobacco and a bottle of whisky if you'll sign.'

George thought fast. As a fisherman he earned about £1 a week and he had a wife and family to keep. This was too good to be true. He signed.

George's story: 'As we were going out of the dock the skipper heard of a ship that had landed a catch that day that had sold for £500. That was a record trip from Iceland. Our skipper had high hopes of doing the same. That cheered us up a bit with visions of a nice bit to pick up when we came home. We little knew how long that was to be…

'We made for the Faroes in a bitter cold wind. The weather was terribly rough. After battling across that treacherous sea we eventually arrived at the Faroes and the skipper decided to have a shot.

'We shot our lines to try our luck and after three hours of trying did not catch anything.'

For the skipper this was just not good enough. A hot headed, impatient man, he wanted action. There was, he reasoned, no point in hanging around. 'That's it, we're off to Iceland,' he declared. Like it or not, the crew had to do what they were told. Despite worsening weather they hauled their nets a final time and set off northwards, arriving on Saturday 16 November.

'Off to Iceland we went in a raging gale. How we ever got there in that sea I don't know. It was snowing, blowing and freezing, My word, it was cold. When we arrived off Iceland it was too rough to fish. We had tried to put in at a fjord for shelter. When we tried to get out again we could not. Every time we were beaten back again. The seas were mountainous. It was three days before we could leave.

'We eventually got out and started to fish. It was hopeless. The wind blew terribly and the sea tossed us about like a cork. We tried to get back to the fjord but could not. We struggled and fought with that sea but it was no use and we could not secure shelter.

'We shipped sea upon sea and almost turned over. It was snowing and freezing. We could not see anything. We made desperate efforts to reach that fjord but all in vain. We had shipped so much water that the ship was at a perilous angle. All at once she shipped a 'blinder', a proper broadside which swept away the wheelhouse, compass and all.

'This, I thought, was the end...'

The weather showed no mercy. Heavy seas smashed over the vessel as she fought to survive, helpless in a storm of terrifying intensity.

She rolled, pitched and heaved, thrown around a vast wasteland of northern waters, her crew, like the vessel herself, fighting for their lives.

Among them was John Brown, a 27-year-old hand who would later recount his story to a reporter on the Grimsby News...

John's story: 'The water rose right on our quarters, came over upon us and dropped fair on to the bridge, carrying it entirely away, with the wheel, the main gaff, the mizzen boom, the cabin skylight, the top of the engine room skylight, part of the cabin door, a clock barometer and all three compasses, boats, sails, spares, gear etc and completely filling the cabin and engine room with water with the result that the fires were put out.'

There were no lights, and in the pitch darkness men clung on to anything they thought secured in an attempt to prevent themselves being flung around the cabin and deck. The engine room was now half filled with water and in the cabin men were waist deep. They were terrified and helpless, at the mercy of nature at her wildest.

And in her hour of crisis the spectre of death loomed over the Sando.

George's story: 'We had to chop away our gear or we would certainly have gone down. One poor chap (William Brown) had his head cut clean from his shoulders and the body was washed overboard. We had to cling to anything we could to prevent being swept away, too.

'We had to do something and do it quickly so we tried to pump out the engine room. We found the pumps were choked and the plates had shifted. We started to bale out with buckets passed one to the other from top to bottom.

'The water was warm through the fires being put out. We had to chain gang the buckets. After a while the man at the top collapsed through cold. We put him in the warm water to bring him round. He was frozen. Another man took his place. The same thing happened to him. So it went on all through the night. We were all dead beat next day. We had no food or anything to warm us up a little...'

For hour after hour they worked, desperate in their attempt to remain alive, each and every man praying that they could clear the engine room of water and re-start the engine. To a man they were bruised and battered after being flung around by the huge seas. But they dare not rest, not for one moment could they cease working. To do so would be fatal.

Eventually they managed to lift the stoke hold plates and clear the pumps, letting the water out of the cabin for the pumps to take up. Still the storm raged, showing no signs of abating. They had no light, no heat, no food and no fire. They were exhausted, frozen to the bone. And they knew that try as they might there was no one who could help them but themselves.

All experienced seamen, they knew that a key factor in their fight to survive was to keep the Sando's *head to wind, dodging the storm. It was a belief that was to be shattered by the skipper who declared suddenly: 'I'm going to turn her round and let her run with the wind...'*

The crew erupted, unanimous in their opposition. It was then that Bill Harris, the mate, spoke up. He knew the consequences of such action having experienced them at first hand and seeing his ship lost.

'Look here, if the skipper does this we will never see Grimsby again. In a sea like this we will not see a ship to help us. The only vessel that comes this way is the mail boat once a year.'

But the skipper had other views. He refused to budge. 'I am master of this ship and I shall do as I decide,' he bawled, his voice and manner leaving them in no doubt of his intentions.

George's story: 'There was no more to be said. We decided to work with him.

'So he turned her round and we feared the worst. She began to go we knew not where, pitching and tossing. It was cruel. Shipping sea upon seas we were wet through to the skin.'

John's story: 'While the water was in the engine room the engineer went down and turned off eight gallons of oil so that when the water was baled out the oil, as it spread, had the effect of calming the water around us.

'We got up steam again and made for Iceland, which was occasionally visible through driving snow. We got into Faksrud Fjord at about six o'clock. It was blowing very hard and freezing so the vessel was covered with ice.

'It was next to impossible to stand on deck and with our clothes being wet they actually froze hard upon us...'

In a final act of desperation Skipper Cutts blew a long solitary blast on the whistle in the hope that someone might hear and investigate.

It was a vain hope, but in the event proved a turning point in their fortunes. Icelandic villagers heard them, put to sea in a skiff and went to investigate.

George's story: 'When they saw our plight they came aboard and took charge of the ship and cast our anchor over the side. Some of them went ashore and brought back corn with which they rubbed us and they made a fire which was a welcome sight.'

Then they began to struggle to make the ship ready to return to England. Success in obtaining a new compass turned to failure when there was no one who was able to correctly adjust it. Then, on 15 December a new plan of action was agreed – they all wrote letters home and engaged an Icelander to walk to Reykjavik some 330 miles distant to deliver them to a mail boat. His pay – about £3.50.

Meanwhile, in Grimsby initial concern that nothing had been heard from the Sando *for several weeks grew in its intensity. But gradually came the realisation that hope was gone. Wives accepted that they had become widows, children that they were orphans.*

But one woman clung to her belief that they were still alive. George Clifford's wife was adamant that this was so, despite what others told her, a belief reinforced she said by a strange dream she had shortly after the vessel was reported missing. In it she believed she saw her husband standing by her bedside and saying 'they'll send a ship out for us and I'll be all right.'

When insurance money was offered she refused it saying there was no need for it to be paid. And while others mourned she simply waited.

John's story: 'There were no other means of taking the package than to walk on account of the rough mountainous road he had to traverse. Sometimes he would have to pick his way surrounded by the frozen snow along the narrow ledge of a high, almost perpendicular rock where there wasn't sufficient room for a pony to go.'

Against all the odds the messages got through, the dog team being found although the Icelander who was delivering them died in a blizzard. The news was received in Grimsby two months later on St Valentine's Day and the Sando's *owners, the White Star Fishing Company, acted swiftly. A sister vessel, the* Sudero, *was dispatched on a rescue mission. But even then the drama was not complete.*

John's story: 'Just as it was becoming light I heard a steamer's whistle. We hurried down to the pier and sure enough we saw a steamer coming up the fjord and found to be the *Sudero*. We shouted to those on her to come and bring us off, but they were all so mad with joy at sight of the other vessel that there was no making them hear for a long time and it was not until they noticed us on the pier that they sent a boat to fetch us.

'The *Sudero* was covered in ice along every rope and spar – in plenty of places it was a couple of feet thick – and she was in fact smothered with ice.

'With the water getting below we understood the men had had to sleep in their bunks with great icicles hanging from the crevices all around them.

'It took us a couple of days to knock all the ice off the vessel, for on some parts it was as thick as a man's waist. If we had left it as it was she would most likely have become top heavy with ice...'

At last everything was made ready and the vessels began to move out. But twice the weather worsened and they were forced to return. Finally, conditions improved sufficiently for them to escape what was later described as 'that forsaken country'.

George's story: 'After three weeks of battling our way across 2,000 miles of rough sea we arrived in Grimsby amid scenes of great joy. A vast crowd came to welcome us home.

'We had long since been given up for lost. In fact the "widow" of one of the crew had married again. It was not the wife of the poor chap we lost. Things don't work out that way.

'My wife was so sure we would return she refused to accept the insurance money offered her. People used to point to her and whisper to one another "look, there is that poor woman who does not believe that her husband is drowned".

'Yet when she heard we were in dock she broke down and was unable to come to make sure...'

Heroes of the trawler fleet

For the crew of the *Staxton Wyke* there was little else to do but relax. The voyage was almost over. Hull was only a few hours away. The vessel, under Skipper Andrew Whitely, was sailing easily on a light sea, although surrounded by dense fog. There was a mood of relaxation, of anticipation. Home after three hard weeks…

Below decks that October night in 1959 Eddie Calvert had gathered his gear together ready for when they docked. Now he rested in his bunk, thumbing through a novel to help fill in the time until he was due to go on watch. It had been a fairly ordinary trip, with nothing outstanding to report.

The trawler was a good, sound vessel, owned by the West Dock Steam Fishing Company of Hull and built at the Beverley yard of Cook, Welton and Gemmell in 1937, originally being called the *Lady Hogarth* until 1946 when it was changed to *Kingston Emerald*. She became the *Staxton Wyke* six years later.

Eddie's mood of wellbeing was shattered as the sound of a klaxon howled through the still night air. 'I thought "Christ, that's close" and went on deck to see what was going on,' he said later. He made it on to the deck at the very moment the 11,000-ton ore carrier *Dalhanna*, on passage from Immingham to Middlesbrough with 8,826 tons of iron ore on board, hit them, ramming straight into the 471-ton trawler and sinking her in just 90 seconds.

'Water was pouring through the portholes on the starboard side. The *Dalhanna* just seemed to stick there in the side for ages, but really it was only for seconds. In fact he was going full astern just before he hit us.

'There was a mad panic. Fortunately we had inflatable lifeboats as there was no time to get a boat out. I got the aft one over and the skipper and mate the forward one. On the raft where I was we managed to get away from the trawler just before she sank.' The men struggled to tie the two rafts together and then drifted helplessly in the fog until the *Dalhanna* drew close to them.

'We tried to paddle her but the swell carried us round in a circle. With another member of the crew I went in and started to swim.' A short time later they were hauled aboard *Dalhanna*, which made a detailed search of the area for five men not accounted for. By now other ships had arrived on the scene, but the search was in vain. None of those who were missing survived.

Mr Calvert, shaken but otherwise unharmed, returned to sea after a brief rest and a year later was sailing as bosun in another Hull vessel, the *St Hubert*.

'I was after a mate's job and went on the trip to see what I was made of,' he later explained. He did well on the voyage – to the White Sea – and his efforts earned him an excellent recommendation from the skipper to the trawler's owners. He did not sail again on the *St Hubert*, staying ashore as she left St Andrew's Dock with a glowing reference for a job on the almost new *Prince Charles*. And it was not long before Mr Calvert again saw tragedy at sea.

In August 1960, when the *Prince Charles* was off the Norwegian Coast – the same area as the *St Hubert* – came an incident in which men displayed the highest courage. Strong winds buffeted the vessels but conditions were still workable and fishing operations continued normally around the clock.

On the *St Hubert* the big talking point among the crew was a mystery object they had trawled up three days earlier, a five-foot long cylindrical canister partially covered in concrete. It had cascaded with the catch on to the deck, been swept clear of the mass of wriggling fish and dragged to a safe area with the intention of dumping it away from the fishing grounds.

Inevitably, the object began to fade as a subject for discussion. Most agreed that it was probably a mine, for it was not uncommon for trawlers to bring them to the surface. Certainly no one thought there was any danger while the object lay on the deck. And then it started ticking.

Seconds later the mine exploded with a deafening roar, wreaking havoc on the trawler. The foredeck was wrecked. Hatches were blown open and most of the port side was ripped away.

On the bridge Skipper George Ness received terrible injuries, half his face being torn away as the windows blew in. With the mate dead and the skipper fighting for his life, but still determined to remain in control of his vessel, the bosun tried to run before the gale, coping for six hours before the weather proved too strong an opponent and forced them to abandon ship. Nearby the *Prince Charles* stood guard, alerted to what had happened by radio.

'When we got to her the wind was about force eight. All her port side had been blown away. There was nothing left standing on deck. All the bridge windows had gone and the skipper was very badly injured, but we were still able to talk to him on the radio,' said Mr Calvert.

'They tried to plug the hole in the hull but it was not very successful and water was going in, even washing fish out of the fishroom and back into the sea. We radioed a doctor but he would not come out – he wanted us to go into Norway.'

Despite their efforts to save her the *St Hubert* was doomed. Battered by the waves she started to go under. Fighting the agony of his appalling injuries Skipper Ness repeatedly asked about the safety of his crew.

The cook, William Adam, told of moments of great heroism. 'The skipper was very weak and seemed to have no blood left in him. They lowered him into a lifeboat and he was still asking if the crew were all right.'

In the rafts the men pulled their way from the side of their stricken vessel as she lay over, fighting to clear her for fear of being sucked down with her.

Then, in another moment of great courage Skipper Bernard Wharam of the *Prince Charles* intervened, taking a calculated risk in a bid to rescue them. Edging towards the *St Hubert* he managed to get in close enough for a line to be thrown to the men in the rafts.

Among the first to be hauled to safety was Skipper Ness, who was immediately given fresh bandages. But the ordeal was too much. He died within 15 minutes of going on board. Fifteen days later in the calm of Hull Coroner's Court tribute was paid to the heroism of Skipper Ness whose actions were said to be 'in the best traditions of trawler fishing.'

The coroner told the hearing: 'I would like to put on record his bravery. Although nearly half his face was blown away he continued to command the sinking trawler with his thoughts always for his ship and crew.'

And from Mr Calvert, who was with Skipper Ness when he died, came the last word: 'He just kept asking me – "are the lads all right?"'

Trawlers sank in sight of home

For the men who crewed the trawlers which left the Humber ports for some of the world's most hostile waters death was a part of life.

These were unsung heroes, the last of the great hunters who battled against appalling conditions to bring home the fish suppers enjoyed by millions. It was a harsh, mean and above all dangerous job, one which saw hundreds of men killed and thousands of children left without fathers.

Those who worked in fishing accepted the danger as part of their life. But on leaving northern waters they could at least expect to be sailing home to safer seas. But not always. Here are the stories of two vessels which set off for home, but never made it – sinking within feet of the fish dock.

It was dark, yet clear. A crisp winter's night with scarcely a breath of wind. On the streets and terraces of Hessle Road the crystal frost shimmered below the yellow street lights. And in the pubs and clubs they sipped their first pints at the start of an evening's drinking.

On the river, just off the fish dock, the trawler *Edgar Wallace* awaited her turn to pass through the lock gates, moored and riding easily on a light swell. Around her the lights from the vessels peppered the inky blackness. And her crew relaxed, eager to be ashore after a trip that had taken in the whole of the festive season.

Men packed their gear, calling out excitedly to each other as they prepared to dock. Three weeks in northern waters were behind them. Ahead lay three days at home. The trip had hardly been pleasant. They had sailed just four days before Christmas, had braved day after day of gales and raging seas. But despite the hazards and the discomforts they had hauled aboard 1,700 kits of fish.

At last it was over. Now came the pay-off, the chance to meet families and old friends, to celebrate – belatedly – Christmas and the New Year. But that calmness, the anticipation of what was to be that night, was suddenly shattered. For the *Edgar Wallace*,

The Kingston Peridot *was one of the three Hull trawlers lost with 58 men in January and February 1968. The tragedy led to new safety measures being introduced for vessels fishing northern waters.*

without warning, keeled over within yards of the dock entrance and sank. And with her went the lives of 15 men.

One of only three survivors, cook Clarry Wilcockson was later to recall a sudden jerk as the trawler hit a sandbank. Yet seconds later she moved back into the channel and righted in deep water.

But again she hit the sand. Only this time she keeled over to an acute angle, one from which she could not recover. Heavy with fish the trawler carried on moving further and further over. Nothing could have saved her.

'I knew at once things were serious and I made my move. I scrambled out on to the top of the galley which was in the afterpart of the vessel. When I got on top I took one of the lifeboats which were kept there and climbed the mizzen mast. I knew she was sinking but you have to keep your head in such situations,' said Clarry.

In the blackness of the night men panicked – and died, many screaming as they realised they were trapped below, unable to escape as the chill waters of the Humber raced through the stricken vessel.

Above, Mr Wilcockson fought for his life, feeling the trawler sliding further and further over until he lost his grip, the swirling waters pulling him away. And still he fought, managing to grab a lifebelt and pull it around him, trapping his hands in its rope.

'I didn't know where to swim, to go to the Yorkshire side of the Humber or Lincolnshire,' he recalled years later.

But his efforts were in vain – the tide carried him upstream. As he drifted he saw the lights of a passing ship and called out desperately in the hope his cries would alert her crew. And back came a voice, faint yet still discernible telling him to keep on calling. But Clarry could not reply. He had passed out.

He awoke to the glare of electric lamps in a ward at the Goole Bartholomew Hospital, some 20 miles away from where the vessel sank. He was later to learn that he had been pulled to safety in the middle of the river by the man who had heard his cries as he floated helplessly.

Another survivor, Mr W. Cameron, told reporters: 'I saw eight or nine men swept away in a flash. I couldn't do anything to help them. They just vanished into the blackness.' As news of the tragedy swept Hull crowds gathered on the quayside of St Andrew's Dock peering into the gloom. As dawn broke they saw just the foremast of the vessel jutting out of the Humber's waves.

Disaster in the Humber

The loss of the *Edgar Wallace* tragedy was still fresh in the memories of many when, just four years later, history – and tragedy – repeated themselves and in almost exactly the same place. 8 March 1939 saw the *Lady Jeanette* return from Iceland after 15 days at sea. As she waited her turn to enter the fish dock she sank, without warning.

A massive rescue operation was immediately mounted, the rescue fleet including tugs and the ferry boat *Wingfield Castle*. They found men clinging for their lives on to the side of the vessel. Some were actually discovered standing on her upturned keel. But for nine members of the crew the trip was their last – they perished within yards of safety and home.

Heroes of sea and air

The word spread rapidly through the bustling streets and busy alehouses of Grimsby, sending men, women and children hurrying to the nearby pontoon to join an excited crowd of dock workers and fishermen.

It was a hot and humid Friday morning in the late summer of 1874 and the normal bustle of dockside business halted as excitement mounted. At the centre of attention was the fishing smack *Grand Charge*, back from a North Sea trip with a 'catch' that would bring members of its crew praise from a foreign government.

The saga began on 31 August in Calais, France when a young and respected aeronaut named Jules Duruof and his wife Caroline were to be the star attraction of an annual fête along with their balloon, *Le Tricolore*.

Duruof was well known for his flying exploits, having built up a formidable reputation as an aeronaut and adventurer. During the siege of Paris in 1863 he had maintained communications between the city and the outer world by means of balloon post. In a flying career which was much admired the intrepid Duruof had made about 60 flights, a remarkable record at a time when an aeronaut had no means of steering his balloon and could control height only by jettisoning ballast to ascend or discharging gas to descend.

At Calais Duruof and his wife made careful preparations for their flight above the town, an event which according to the schedule which would take place at 4pm. But no one reckoned on what the weather might bring. By the appointed hour a strong wind was blowing in a direction which would take the balloon on a north-easterly course over open sea. The likelihood of the couple being able to descend on land was slight.

Friends were adamant that the flight should not take place, but the dashing Duruof paid no heed, that is until the Mayor of Calais stepped in and forbade them to go ahead. Reluctantly they agreed, but left the balloon inflated so that an ascent might be made the following day if conditions allowed.

Reckless though Duruof tended to be he was certainly no coward and easily took offence that evening when he overheard local people accusing him of not having the courage to take to the air. His honour, he decided, was at stake, so together with his wife he secretly returned to the balloon, climbed into its basket and set off. It was a reckless and foolish thing to do. Dusk was fast approaching and within minutes of rising from the ground the balloon was heading towards the North Sea.

But Duruof was unperturbed. He would later write of a night which passed without incident as the craft continued on its journey trailing a 70-metre rope below it. The idea was that when the end of the rope touched the water Duruof would throw out ballast to recover height. But his luck was running out.

When daylight came he began to realise that his position was hopeless, the balloon being carried far away from land. He decided the only hope was to descend, try to land on the water and hope that help would arrive from one of several vessels he had spotted, most of them fishing smacks on the Dogger Bank. The landing was a good one, the balloon dropping gently onto the water where it floated, pushed along by the wind and dragging the car with its occupants behind it.

The sea was rough, and the wind increasing in intensity, and for the next hour both Duruof and his wife were drenched by wave after wave sweeping over the car as they clung on desperately to the balloon gear. But help was on the way, their plight having been spotted by the *Grand Charge*. Skipper William Oxley and the vessel's mate, James Bascombe, went to their rescue in a small boat.

A later report of the incident recorded their bravery: 'The adjective intrepid, already applied to the aeronauts, can equally be applied to these hardy fishermen who had to navigate their small boat in a high running sea. Risky as this was, the danger was vastly increased when they approached the plunging, swirling balloon with its entanglement of ropes and other gear.

'By superb seamanship and great daring the task was accomplished. The aeronauts were got into the boat which was safely rowed back to the smack. Here the cabin was made over to the rescued couple and hot drinks, food and blankets provided.'

In Grimsby the Duruofs could not offer enough praise for the fishermen. Madame Duruof presented her pearl and ruby ring to the mate who had managed to lift her from the balloon car and into the safety of the boat.

The French Government, too, was warm in its praise, presenting gold medals and monetary awards to the skipper and mate. And later that year a fête was held in Calais in honour of the skipper and mate, raising £50 for them.

The story did not end there. The balloon was eventually picked up about 100 miles from Norway by the Hull smack *Zedora,* which landed it at Hull a few days later.

Index